About the Author

I have lived as an adult Christian for over fifty years, working as a barrister, as a local judge in Liverpool, before becoming a judge in the Family Division. For forty-six years of that time, I lived with my family in one of the more deprived areas of a northern city, trying to fulfil a vocation as lawyer, family man, lay preacher and whatever else has come my way. This is a reflection with the benefit of hindsight and experience of what being a Christian on the front line might be about.

The Salt of The Earth?

Mark Hedley

The Salt of The Earth?

Olympia Publishers
London

www.olympiapublishers.com
OLYMPIA PAPERBACK EDITION

A CIP catalogue record for this title is
available from the British Library.

ISBN: 978-1-80074-577-3

First Published in 2023

Olympia Publishers
Tallis House
2 Tallis Street
London
EC4Y 0AB
Printed in Great Britain

Dedication

Fulfilling a vocation is a family effort in which the total is greater than the sum of the parts. This book is dedicated to Erica and to Mike, Anna, Ste and Pete, who have sustained me with love and challenge over nearly all (in Erica's case), or much of my adult life.

Acknowledgements

This book has been read by a number of friends who have helpfully commented on its contents, and in several ways have significantly affected its final form, but the life behind it has been supported by numerous friends, colleagues and fellow Christian disciples to whom I owe a debt greater than they would know or I could repay.

CHAPTER 1

INTRODUCTION: SETTING THE SCENE

Today, in those parts of the Earth where western Christians live, we describe ourselves as living in a secular culture. By that perhaps we mean a society in which there is no essential requirement for or acknowledgment of a spiritual (and in particular a transcendent) dimension. Whereas even the atheists of three hundred years ago would have regarded themselves as living in a Christian culture, the Christians of today find themselves living in a secular culture. I am wary of this description "secular culture" but not only can I find no better phrase, it is one that our modern culture has used to describe itself. We were often reminded as judges of the Family Division of the High Court that we were secular judges sitting in a secular court and administering secular law.

If indeed we were to go back three hundred years in our history, we would find that the ethical issues which occupy us today were all essentially framed in religious language. It was religion (Christianity) that was the essential source and arbiter of ethics. That began to change in the 18th century as scientific experiment and thought, and the philosophical approaches that grew from it, began to question the prevailing religious certainties. It has been described as the Age of Enlightenment. It created a dichotomy (which many now see as false) between scientific experiment and rational thinking based on evidence on the one hand and the dogmatic certainties of religion on the other. That process has continued apace ever since.

We find ourselves living in an age which confronts ethical issues that have not existed before in many areas of our personal lives and in our society and we have had to deal with them without recourse to the old certainties. We struggle with issues of personal values and morality, social justice and social control, of our worldwide responsibilities including climate change and obvious health and economic inequalities, as well as matters of international peace and security. Of course many of these issues have been around for as long as the human race has existed but in a world of easy global communication they confront us in a way that is unique in history. Moreover, our sheer scientific and technical skills pose questions that we had never before had to address whether in the great issues of the creation of life or the postponing or bringing about death or more mundane matters of economic judgment.

That is uncomfortable and, no doubt, is part of the reason why many find fundamentalism in all its aspects attractive — it seems to offer a way through. As ever, nothing is quite as simple as that. We are discovering that whilst our technological skills develop apace, our ethical skills do not and we are left with, if anything, a widening gap between the two in many areas of modern life. This is the world in which the modern Western Christian has to live and it is not an easy place in which to do so.

Over the last hundred years or so, our society has made huge progress in recognising and articulating human rights, from votes for women, through the experiences of two world wars and up to the issues that dominate public thinking today. Indeed, in any particular situation, our society is quite proficient in spelling out the rights of all those involved. And we should be glad of that.

However, we are much less good and much less equipped at resolving conflicts of rights as, for example, the rights of parents as against the State to decide for their children in a medical dispute. This is rather vividly shown by the European Convention on Human Rights itself (or indeed any similar Convention around today) in that whilst rights are clearly spelt out, conflicts of rights are not dealt with beyond an acknowledgement that one person's rights may have to be restricted to accommodate the rights of another.

Our law has arrived at this position. Where there is a conflict of rights, one must weigh all the issues that tend both for and against the rights of each person involved and, then having done that, must strike a "fair balance" using the yardstick of "proportionality" — balancing the harm done by restricting one set of rights against the benefits achieved by upholding the other. This is not a recipe for clarity, certainty or consistency. In the Old Testament, we find this comment in relation to one period in the history of the Jewish People:

"In those days, there was no king in Israel; all the people did what was right in their own eyes."[1]

This was not a description of widespread freedom in society but of anarchy.

In many ways, those are the marks of a secular society in which all are essentially free to say, believe and do what is right in their own eyes, subject only to such consensus or majority opinion as can be framed by a law. It is not surprising that this should produce uncertainty. It is not surprising that the sheer complexity of our society should drive people to single-issue campaigns or to the toleration of only a limited set of opinions, which are at least clear and manageable even if they do not

---

[1] Judges 21 v 25.

13

confront the problems of conflict of rights.

That is the society in which modern Western Christians now find themselves living, and it is not a comfortable place to be. This book is about trying to live with integrity in such a culture whilst retaining with integrity the Christian faith and all that that implies.

I have worked in the law since 1971. I have been a conscious Christian since 1958 and a Reader[2] in the Church of England since 1975. I lived in the Everton district of Liverpool from 1974 to 2020, having been involved there since 1971. I have been a husband since 1973 and a father since 1975. I have taken my share of responsibility in the charitable sector. These comprise distinct areas of life: family, work, church and community. The priority between them has been unclear and sometimes controversial. What has, in fact, happened is that I have lived somewhat towards the edge of each, though seemingly committed to all. It breeds that great frustration of not quite being able to do anything as well as one would have liked because of the pressing need not to be swamped.

My working life has involved being both a barrister and a judge. The legal profession has a strong code of ethics and demanding standards of professional conduct, most especially amongst the judiciary, but there is no spiritual, let alone transcendent, dimension to it. In that, it mirrors most current professional bodies and the intrinsic thought of our society.

My aim is not to provide answers, as they will be as varied as those who choose to read this book. My aim is to encourage the reader, to provoke thought and to stimulate him or her to progress their own consideration of their calling, together with

---

[2] This is the order of authorized lay ministers in the Anglican Church, licensed to preach, teach, lead worship and share in the leadership of a local church.

the consequences of doing so, within the Kingdom of God.

This book essentially assumes the truth of the Christian faith in the sense that there is no overt intention of writing apologetics. Its purpose is simply to try to demonstrate to Christians, or to any thinking seriously about the Christian faith, how the Christian life might really be lived with integrity in a secular culture.

As I have reflected over many years now on that life with its challenges and frustrations, I have concluded that church leaders and theologians may not be able to engage with these tensions quite as fully as many laypeople actually experience them. It is fashionable to characterize the church as both "the gathered community" and also "the dispersed community". We can be, and often are, well equipped for being the gathered community, which is, of course, the sharp end of most priestly vocation: worship, the life of the church and the service it can offer to those amongst whom it is placed.

The actual experience of many Christians is, however, often quite different. For us, the greater part of our life is on our own in the dispersed community. No doubt we are cared for and prayed for, though many of us will go months, even years, at a time without hearing our field of work featuring in Sunday intercessions. The question is how we can be equipped and sustained to serve as effective members of that dispersed community. We spend much of our lives in situations that church leaders will never experience. It is not that we have been abandoned to our own devices (though it can sometimes feel like that), but I have been driven to the view that we must train and teach ourselves and especially learn from those Christians who have walked the same road as we do.

In one sense, of course, the answer is quite simple. Christians have the two great commandments: to love God with every part of our being and to love our neighbours as ourselves. We are to give primacy to our God and parity to our neighbours. I do not want in any way to detract from what continues to lie at the heart of what living as a Christian is all about. Yet it is in the outworking of it that the difficulties arise. How do you give primacy to a God whom our society generally either rejects or ignores? How do you love your neighbour when their chosen lifestyle and values are seriously at variance with ours? It is engaging with those kinds of questions that has provoked my writing this book.

I do not doubt that there is a proper and important place within the Christian community for clergy and theologians, as indeed I will repeatedly acknowledge in this book. They have space for reflection and thought, which is denied to others (including judges) and which is a key ingredient of good teaching. However, much of what I have read and heard from them has the feel of coming from an observer rather than a participant in our secular society. This is a book written from the inside with all the limitations that it may bring. It is also written from the perspective of one convinced of Jesus' words, and sometimes weighed down by them, that much is required of those to whom much is given.

Much of what I have learnt about what it means to be a Christian lawyer, I have learned from other Christian lawyers, just as much of what I have learnt about living the faith with integrity in our secular culture, I have learned from others who have tried to do the same. Some of those are people from history, some I have known but who have since died, and some are still alive. I must, however, mention one who is no longer alive and whose name will be known only to very few. Roger Dowley was a solicitor who decided early in his professional life to devote work, home and family to the East End of London long before any part of it became fashionable. He sought throughout his life to read and hear the Scriptures in the context of that experience. I had already made a similar commitment in Liverpool when I first met him, but his insights and his undeservedly little-known work "The Lost Bequest"[3] have been hugely influential in my thinking. Roger Dowley could never have been accused of courting publicity or popularity, but a proper acknowledgement of his role in my life is the very least that I can offer here.

I am no theological expert. Certainly, I have the benefit of experience, and I have the benefit, as a Reader, of having tried in my preaching over forty years to hold that experience in constructive tension with Christian teaching. As I grew up in central London, I was soaked with the preaching of John Stott and the writings of C.S. Lewis and many others. I have maintained my reading, though necessarily it is highly selective, and I have borrowed shamelessly from the thoughts and insights of others, usually, but by no means always, Christians. I am not a scholar in the sense of being able to reference the origins of my thoughts that I have long since committed to a subconscious that has no index of authors. Whilst I have tried to acknowledge sources where I can, my position is well caught by words used by Bishop John Taylor in his introduction to his book "The Go-Between God"[4]:

"I apologise to all who while reading the pages that follow will have the sensation of having heard it before, and confess that very often the reason will be the plain fact that I am a borrower and retailer of other men's ideas."

Yet whilst this book does not pretend to be a work of

---

[3] First edition 1984 and commemorative edition 2004 — ECUM.
[4] SCM Press 1972.

scholarship, it does, I trust, have some intellectual rigour. Being a reflection on a personal journey and the issues that have been thrown up in it, it necessarily draws on my personal experience for illustration, but it is not intended as a memoir or autobiography. I am, therefore, aware of one real danger.

I have pursued a professional career, and most of what I have to offer is influenced by that. As this is essentially a personal reflection, it will inevitably have a professional flavour. There is, therefore, a real risk that this will be seen as being for professionals only. That is decidedly not my purpose. I have lived and worshipped for long enough in my corner of Liverpool to have fully appreciated that God works through all his children irrespective of education, status, ability or any other human classification. What lies behind my thinking is available and relevant to anyone who finds themselves deeply immersed in our culture in whatever capacity. I would want to urge any who read this not just to take it at face value but to apply what is read to the reader's own life. It would be presumptuous of me to say how that should work out in the lives of others. In any event, as I have said, there would be as many answers as there are readers. Each of us is answerable to God for the life that is lived. Each of us must therefore decide how our life is to be lived. If this book can make any significant contribution to that, I will have had my reward.

So how are we to go about this task? That is the question that this book seeks to address. We need to start with an acknowledgement that the earth is the Lord's and everything in it, coupled with some thoughts on the implications of that. We then need to understand our status within the created order as children of God before going on to consider our specific place (or vocation) in that order as the servants of God. Following from that, I want to reflect on some of Jesus' metaphors for Christian living — salt, light and yeast — before looking at some biblical models for living — ambassador, steward and tenant. That will highlight some of the tensions that we face, and we need to consider how these can be lived out both in the Christian community and amongst those with whom we work and share our lives. In the light of all that, we should consider the resources available to us and our place within the local church. That is followed by three reflections on how Scripture may look and sound different to us because of our individual experience.

The Christian life is, however, risky and open to mistakes. This book will not be free of them, but the risk of getting it wrong is a necessary condition for any venture, and the avoidance of mistake is never a satisfactory excuse for not trying. Nevertheless, please enter with your eyes wide open!

CHAPTER 2

CREATION: THE EARTH IS THE LORD'S

That great bishop Stuart Blanch, initially of Liverpool and then of York, was once challenged in a public lecture to summarize the Bible in a sentence. His trademark angelic smile heralded this response: "I can do better than that; I can do it in four words — the Sovereign Lord reigns." For me, then a young law student, that reply opened a new line of thought. Here was God, not just Lord of the Church but Lord of the whole created order. Here was God not just concerned about the work and witness of the Church but concerned about every aspect of his creation. Here was God who loved not only those who responded to him but loved and cared for the whole created order. It was Stuart Blanch who first anchored for me any mature understanding of the gospel firmly in the Old Testament. That was in part in his preaching and in his writing but also in a public lecture series that he gave in Liverpool Cathedral. The one that sticks in my mind, which was transformative of my thinking and which may well have given rise to the exchange above, was "The Affluent Society in the light of Amos". The church, he asserted, was born not at Pentecost but in the call of Abraham in Genesis 12. The promises to Abraham were promises to all the world — "I will indeed bless you, and I will make your offspring as numerous as the stars of heaven and the sand that is on the seashore. And your offspring shall possess the gate of their enemies, and by your offspring shall all the nations of the earth gain blessing for themselves, because you have obeyed my voice."[5]

This continuity from Abraham is at the heart of Tom Wright's magisterial study of Paul. For Paul, Christianity was not a new religion, but the fulfilment of God's promises (including those to Abraham) in that faith reimagined in the light of Jesus the Messiah of God. It was not that God had sent a saviour to His People but that God had come as the Messiah. In Jesus, so Paul understood, "all the fullness of God was pleased to dwell... In whom are hidden all the treasures of wisdom and knowledge."[6] It follows that any mature reflection in the New Testament must be had in the context of an understanding of the Old Testament. The one does not supplant the other but fulfils it.

The whole Bible is the story of salvation, and every part of that story has to be understood in the context of the whole. The story starts with the perfect creation that is then spoiled by sin and human implication in sin. The resulting moral and spiritual mess is illustrated both in the story of the Flood and of the Tower of Babel. The rest of the Bible is the story of God's rescue of his creation. It runs from the call of Abraham, through the story of the Jewish People, the prophets and finds its climax in Jesus and the gospel. It continues through his resurrection and Pentecost and the spread of the gospel throughout the world. It ends with the judgment of the world and the restored perfect creation that forms the climax of the Book of Revelation. We are now the inheritors of those promises to Abraham.

This understanding of God's relationship to the whole of the created order means that there is no part of human life with which God is not concerned. If that be right, it means that there is no

---

[5] Genesis 22 v 17–18.
[6] Colossians 1 v 19; 2 v 3.

part of human life — and indeed of the whole created order — with which Christians should not be involved. And if that be right, then we might expect to find God working through Christians in all sorts of surprising and unexpected places — even, as I was to discover, in the secular world of the law.

Yet all that should not have come to me as the surprise that it did. After all, God had created humanity as social beings. We need, in order to thrive, personal relationships with other humans. The successful hermit is a rarity. At the same time, it is apparent that humanity finds doing wrong easier than doing right, especially when the pressure is on. Therefore, to sustain social life, some degree of restraint and regulation is required. This can be done by the power of naked force or by law oiled by Justice. Although history has plenty of examples of the former, God has given us the latter, so we should not be surprised to find Christians, even me, involved in it. I think that you can and should construct a parallel piece of reasoning to account for Christian involvement in every human activity, however major or minor, paid or unpaid, public or out of sight that role might be.

It is, of course, easier to do in some areas rather than others. To see God's creative drive being worked out in medicine, teaching, or social care may not be too difficult. Those in education see that as a means of stabilizing the society in which otherwise strength alone would prevail. All those involved in care know that dignity in adversity is what keeps the human spirit aflame. It is also probably true of government. It is less clear in trade, commerce, transport or entertainment. Yet the God revealed in the Old Testament is passionate about fair business and trade. What about this, for instance — "The voice of the Lord cries in the city… Hear O tribe and assembly of the city! Can I forget the treasures of wickedness in the house of the wicked and the scant measure that is accursed? Can I tolerate wicked scales and a bag of dishonest weights? Your wealthy are full of violence; your inhabitants speak lies, with tongues of deceit in their mouths." [7] And there is more where that came from. What happens in everyday living matters to this God. Again, God created the world for us to enjoy, one in which we could and should travel. All those involved in public transport know that the ability to travel and mix is what creates communities rather than ghettos. In days of global warming, however, this is not an easy balance to find, but it is a human (and therefore Christian) responsibility to do so. God delights in joy and laughter and the exploration of emotions; entertainment matters. But this God hates cruelty, deceit and the glorification of sin. Those offer real challenges to Christians in the entertainment industry.

Every so often, this sort of challenge shines through a biblical passage. I remember as a young barrister coming across this passage in Isaiah: "The Lord saw it, and it displeased him that there was no justice. He saw that there was no one, and was appalled that there was no one to intervene." [8] That, of course, can speak not only to a lawyer but also to anyone engaged in public service. There are many such passages, some of which I refer to in this book. However, what struck me was the relationship of all this to the religious life. The Old Testament vision is that life is all of a piece, and every one part is integrated in every other.

The Bible sees each individual human being as a single, complete and integrated entity, what has been described as a "psychosomatic whole". Jewish thought knows nothing of the Greek division of the human being into body, mind and spirit. And just as human beings are seen as a whole, so our life and

---

[7] Micah 6 v 9–12.
[8] Isaiah 59 v 15–16.

worship are to be seen in the same way. That is why we find very strong denunciations in the prophetic writings where these things have got out of sync, and what we do and say is no longer compatible with what we profess in worship. This is powerfully illustrated in Amos, where the prophet lists the injustices in the land and then adds these words of the Lord — "I hate, I despise your festivals, and I take no delight in your solemn assemblies. Even though you offer me your burnt offerings and your grain offerings, I will not accept them... Take away the noise of your songs; I will not listen to the melody of your hearts. But let justice roll down like waters, and righteousness like an ever-flowing stream."[9] Other equally vivid examples are found in Isaiah 1 (where very similar language is used) and 58. I am still astonished by the strength of the language of these passages. They are by no means confined to Amos but bubble up again and again in prophetic thought and writings. Their emphatic assertion that God rejects the worship of those whose lives are a denial of that worship is something that every generation of worshippers should heed. This offers a framework within which we must read the New Testament, all of whose writers had the Old Testament as their Scriptures and all of whom respected its authority. The gospels cannot be fairly read without appreciating both his reverence for the scriptures (the Old Testament, of course) and Jesus' insistence that what we say and believe must be matched by the lives that we live.

All this is not to advocate any particular political approach. It is to demonstrate that, as God has created the world, so he loves it and is concerned in every part of it and requires that that should be the mindset of his People. That is easier said than done in modern Western Christianity. In order to ensure that we do

---

[9] Amos 5 v 21–24.

remain faithful to the mindset required by God, we need to understand the context of the modern Western church so that we can understand why these things may be more difficult than once they were. There is, of course, nothing new in the issue of persuading Christians that God was concerned with every aspect of life and that we should serve him there. That was the thrust in 1797 of William Wilberforce's book — "A Practical View of Christianity" (its short title)[10] — but he was dealing with a quite different context. There, his words were a challenge to "nominal Christians", which really meant the substantial bulk of his society. Our concerns may be the same, but the modern context is different. We may still have "nominal Christians", but our society's thinking is necessarily shaped by a secular culture that questions the place of faith beyond purely personal belief. It is the impact of that culture on the church that is our immediate concern.

I write from a perspective of life-long membership of the Church of England, and that will undoubtedly dictate how I see things. However, not all Christians see things in the same way. As a generalization, it can be said that the church is in decline in the West (unlike, of course, much of the rest of the world where it grows apace) both numerically and in terms of its influence. Church leaders are understandably and rightly concerned to reverse that trend. It is, however, here that difficulties can arise. Our diocesan slogan is "Bigger churches to make a bigger difference". So what is wrong with that? Well, I could argue, although it is a lot less snappy, that the slogan ought to add the words after *churches* "with better discipled members" — which in fairness is what is intended and shown by the diocesan "Rule of Life". However, the problem lies, as it so often does, in the

---

[10] Republished in Hendrickson's Christian Classics 1996.

unspoken message, the spoken message being fine as far as it goes. A truth that is not the whole truth is always at risk of being heard as an untruth.

This slogan potentially carries the implication (though I doubt it is intended to do so) that real Christian ministry lies in the building up of your local church and so in the ministry exercised under its auspices. This was reinforced in a lecture I heard from the incumbent of a large London church. She told us of "the gathered community" — what happened in and around the church — and "the dispersed community" (or, as some refer to it, *the sent community*) — what happened elsewhere, and she referred to some of the interesting jobs and posts and spheres of influence held by members of her congregation. The rest of the lecture then focused on what happened in and around her church. Now it would not be fair to criticize her: that was her job and no doubt the point of the lecture. My point is the unspoken message. In truth, God probably had more scope for action through the dispersed community, but you would not necessarily have appreciated that their service to God, where they were, was actually recognised as an equal part of the ministry of the church, and so it may not have been valued as such.

Of course, that particular judgment may not be entirely fair in that case, but it does illustrate a concern that over-much attention is given by church leaders to what is done through the institutional church and gathered community, and a consequence of that is that those whose time is spent in the dispersed community do not see their work there as a distinctive Christian ministry. This is an issue to which we must return in chapter 4.

Over the years, it has appeared to me that there are two broad traditional metaphors for Christian living. One is sheltering from the world safely protected inside Fortress Church — the City of

God. Although few would actively advocate this metaphor as the whole truth, it is one that has always represented a well-recognised approach. Nor is it wholly false. Of course, we need protection, and of course, we need to retrench from time to time. The early church needed its solid base in Jerusalem, led by James and others, just as it needed the Gentile mission, led by Paul and others. The other metaphor is one of aliens and pilgrims living nomadically in tents as we pass along the journey of life. That metaphor is helpful in emphasising the transitory nature of life and the lack of worldly security that can attend those who faithfully follow Christ, who take up their cross daily to follow him. It has the danger, though, of suggesting that Christian life is lived outside the culture in which we live or the church to which we belong. I hope that we will look more closely at this in chapter 9. The reality is that both metaphors contain elements of truth. As ever, it is using metaphors as illustrations that can lead to understanding rather than confusing metaphor with definition. I need to use metaphor in order to look beyond it for greater understanding rather than using it as a refuge to justify what happens to be congenial to me.

At the same time, the increasing secularization of our culture discourages Christian contribution outside the sphere of personal religious faith. There are many who question the propriety, let alone the relevance, of any distinctive faith contribution in the public square. If that view is now being challenged, then that has been by the rise of Islam as a significant factor in the life of our country. Christians should welcome and encourage that challenge. People of faith are as entitled as those of none to engage in debate in the public square. It is true that we may have to recognise that we need to accommodate our language to the prevailing culture. To use Christian concepts like sin or righteousness or faith or to assume the authority of Scripture in public debate may turn our hearers off, but, as I hope to show later (chapter 7) that accommodation can be attempted without betraying our integrity as Christians. The consequence for Christians has been to induce something that resembles a siege mentality that finds expression in the emphasis on the life of the local church or an almost obsessional focus on personal (and in particular sexual) morality. Now all these, of course, are necessary concerns for Christians so long as they are held in tension with the need for Christians to participate in every aspect of human life, and a recognition that that participation is at least of equal value to ministry pursued through the auspices of the church. I want to examine these issues in more detail later in the book.

This book is not about Christian ministry expressed in and through the local church. The number of such books is legion. My concern is that we should acknowledge in our lives the creator God's love for and involvement in the whole of the created order. We should expect to find Christians — including ourselves — serving God anywhere in that wide arena. Of course, there will be limits, as Christians cannot align themselves with the promotion of wrongdoing. That said, there will remain contentious boundaries: pubs, betting shops, loan companies — the list is probably very long. In that service, we should feel supported and, where possible, equipped by the church to do that as a significant aspect of our lifelong Christian service to God. This book needs to be read from that perspective.

CHAPTER 3

ADOPTION: OUR STATUS IN GOD'S WORLD

We have seen that this world was created by and belongs to God. We should, therefore, not be surprised to find his people involved in every aspect of it or that we may find ourselves involved in something apparently far removed from anything that looks or feels religious. Our concern is how we address that whilst remaining loyal to Our Lord and faithful to his people. We need to start not just by finding a place in God's world but also first by understanding our status as a child of God in that world.

We humans have all been created by God, but to those who serve him, he has given the status of a child of God. In the great Prologue to his Gospel, John writes: "But to all who received him, who believed in his name, he gave the power to become children of God." The question is not whether we can become children of God (for that has been promised to us) but how, for this is the foundation on which everything else is built.

The Bible has a number of pictures to illustrate the making of this relationship between believer and God. It uses "being born again", "being saved", "coming to faith", sometimes called "conversion". No doubt there are other pictures too. One such picture is "adoption", and it is that that I would like to explore. I have three reasons for choosing adoption. First, I have both personal and extensive professional involvement with it and have discovered the richness of the picture in terms of explaining

29

Christian experience. Secondly, some of the other pictures have become, if not discredited, then at least unattractive by the ways in which they have been used and in which they are portrayed in our culture. The third reason is that it answers the question "how", which comes from the Prologue.

It is, however, very important that we do not press the adoption picture too far. It is an illustration and not an allegory. In the world in which Paul used it, or John drew upon it,[11] they were presumably (since Jewish law had no concept of adoption) using Roman law ideas of adoption; we must look at these later. Adoption in English law first came into statutory existence in 1926, and we have had three major Adoption Acts subsequently in 1950, 1976 and 2002. Originally the adoption slogan was "A homeless child for a childless home". Adoption then usually involved babies of single mothers who could not care for them or who were otherwise orphans. The advent of much greater tolerance for single mothers, the contraceptive pill and better health care, as well as legal abortion, dramatically reduced the number of babies available. That idea, however, dominated thinking about adoption until perhaps the 1970s. Adoption then started to become used in Care cases. Nowadays, most children who are adopted have been in State care and are not babies, and many adoptors already have their own children. Adoption is a means by which our society secures permanence for children who are at risk in the care system.

That was the experience of our family. We were local authority foster parents for a while. Then it became clear that two of these children needed permanence, ideally where they were, and so in due course, were adopted into our family. Although the

---

[11] See, for example, Romans 8 v 15, Ephesians 1 v 5, John 1 v 12 or 1 John 3 v 1–2.

legal concept of adoption has effectively remained the same for nearly a hundred years, its social purpose has altered quite a bit. The law may be much the same, but the social context is different.

However, it is important to remember that the British concept of adoption is not shared by most of the world. Not the least is this because of the "compulsory" element, the power of the court to impose adoption on unwilling parents by dispensing with their consent, and thereby effectively causing them to cease to exist legally so far as the child is concerned. Adoption is a picture in the Christian life, I think a very useful picture, but that is what it is and no more. It is, after all, heavily influenced by the culture in which it is practised. The picture generated by the word in this country is not the same as it would be elsewhere, even in Europe.

The world of the New Testament was influenced and often governed by Roman law. Roman courts ensured transparency by building courts without walls so that all proceedings were very public. As the volume of legislation was slight and therefore often well known by its citizens, they were then more likely to know more about the workings of the law and the courts than the modern citizen, who may never encounter a court at all. Yet they live in such a complex legal system that even the professionals cannot know all the detail of the law but, at best, only where to find it.

The process of adoption, known as *adoptio*, was therefore probably well known to most New Testament Christians. It was rooted in the concept of *patria potestas*, the power of the eldest male over the rest of the family, a power so absolute that it included the power to sell into slavery and had, in former times, included a power of life and death. What happened in *adoptio* was that two fathers would agree on an adoption, often for the purpose of providing a male heir for the family without one, and they would then meet before a judge. The adoptee's natural father would then *sell* the child to the father of the other family and then *buy* him back; that would be repeated. It was the third sale that was crucial for, by the Roman law of that time, not only had the power over life and death been abolished but also a man who sold his child three times lost *patria potestas* over him. Thus, on the third *sale,* the child could not be bought back but passed legally into the other family. There was also a provision that, if the child were of sufficient age, he had to consent for the transaction to be legally effective. In Roman law, the adoptee might well have been an adult; a famous historical example of this being the adoption by Julius Caesar of Octavius, who in due course became the Emperor Augustus. Thus, an adoption was effected and was done in public and would become widely known.

The more I have thought about this picture, the more it tells me about the experience of becoming and being a Christian. A father chooses a child as God has chosen me. A father buys (or redeems) a child, as God, through the sacrifice of Jesus on the Cross, has redeemed me. I must agree to this change, for the members of the family of God are all volunteers. I then become a member of the family of God as a permanent fixture. I can remember the moment that it happened for me in 1958, shortly before my twelfth birthday. That will not be everybody's experience. To some, it will come as a dawning realisation that they have been adopted. For others, it will always seem to have been so. God deals with each one as the unique individual that they are. It is a powerful picture.

However, the Roman picture alone was inadequate, for it

conferred *patria potestas* (and thus the right of onward sale) on the adoptive father. There was, at least in law, a real insecurity in the arrangement. This Paul addresses through his knowledge of Jewish law that, whilst having no concept of adoption, did know of life-long guardianship, initially voluntary but, once assumed, enforceable. This enabled Paul, by using the commercial concept of a deposit, to indicate that through the Holy Spirit our inheritance, the permanence of our status as a child of God, is guaranteed — "In him you also, when you have heard the word of truth, the gospel of your salvation, and had believed in him, were marked with the seal of the promised Holy Spirit; this is the pledge of our inheritance towards redemption as God's own people, to the praise of his glory."[12]

Thus, through adoption, we see our status within God's world: a permanent family member as a child of God to share in the inheritance of all God's goodness. The biblical picture of adoption and inheritance is often framed in masculine language — "as sons". Whilst this may simply reflect the culture of the day, it also makes the point that every Christian, male or female, receives the full inheritance of children (as sons did) rather than the lesser inheritance then due to the daughter. That is the position from which we start. This is where we belong in God's world.

A further reason why I find the picture of adoption helpful is that it explains a number of troubling sensations or feelings to which many of us Christians are prone. Have you in a bad period wondered on a Sunday morning, surrounded by bright, cheery worshippers, whether you really belong here at all? Do they really know how you feel and the pressures you are under as you seek to serve God? Have you ever wondered when in some aspect

---

[12] Ephesians 1 v 13–14.

of your life you feel that you have badly let down our God, whether you really are secure in this family forever? And have you sometimes envied the life of those not troubled by the burden of being a Christian and hankered after that life? If so, you are experiencing some of the concerns that often affect adopted people everywhere — do I really belong here for I am so unlike them, am I always going to be allowed to be a member of this family however I behave or what about my original family, even if I know who they are, after all, I am biologically and genetically part of them and not of this? Questions like these, float around often provoked by quite mundane experiences in life. They can be quite disturbing and distressing to experience, especially as most others will not be able to appreciate how the adopted person feels. That is why the slogan "adoption is forever" is so important. Adoption makes you one of the family; in our law, an adopted person is to be treated as though born to the adopters.[13] Nothing can separate you from that. And, as Paul reminds us,[14] God treats us in exactly the same way. The Holy Spirit is our guarantee of permanence in this family, come what may.

There is nothing wrong or unusual with Christians having these feelings or questions: they are to be expected. Of course we will feel a draw to the life from which we have been adopted. As many of us will spend most of our time amongst those who share that life, how could we not have those feelings or questions? If you want an illustration of someone hankering for a life untroubled by the demands of God, go to Psalm 73. I know exactly how the Psalmist feels, just as I appreciate the need always to retain the perspective of eternity. As the Psalmist observes — "but when I thought how to understand this, it

---

[13] See section 67(1) of the Adoption & Children Act 2002.
[14] Ephesians 1.

seemed to me a wearisome task, until I went into the sanctuary of God; then I perceived their end."[15] God knows the tensions we experience, otherwise he would not have expressly had to tell us that we have a "guarantee".

Again, there will be times when we wonder whether we really belong to God's family (these church members seem so different and on such a different plane to us) and, indeed, whether we deserve to be such a member anyway. Adoption, however, is forever. It is a fact unrelated to feelings or to what we deserve. It is a gift freely given, willingly received and then guaranteed for eternity. All this affirms not only our status within God's world, but it is a status that is both inviolate and perpetual.

What does this status mean for us in our lives beyond, of course, a guarantee that we eternally belong in God's family (as if that were not enough!)? For this, we need to go back to the laws and customs that prevailed in the world of the New Testament. As we have seen, Paul, in both Romans and Galatians, calls us "sons of God". This he does to show, not only permanence but also, where in Christ there is neither male nor female, that we shall all receive the full inheritance of God's kingdom just as boys received their father's inheritance. God holds back nothing from his children. Yet Paul also refers to Christians as "slaves of God". That sounds stranger to our ears than it would have done to Paul's hearers. In the ancient world, there might not be much apparent difference in style or dress between a son and an established household slave; indeed, the latter might well have had disciplinary powers over the former and might enjoy a more responsible relationship with the father. Many a slave was more useful than a tiresome teenage child and, if you know Robert Harris's fictional trilogy on Cicero, you have

---

[15] Psalm 73 v 16–17.

an excellent example of this in Cicero's slave-secretary Tiro.[16]

There were, however, real differences between slaves and sons. As Jesus himself put it — "I no longer call you servants [or slaves], because the servant does not know his master's business. Instead, I have called you friends, for everything that I have learned from my father, I have made known to you."[17] Paul too explains the difference between a son and a slave despite the fact that "...As long as the heir is a child, he is no different from a slave, although he owns the full estate."[18] In other words, there is truth in the description of us as a son, just as there is in calling us a slave. It is another example of metaphors increasing understanding so long as they are treated as pictures and no more than that. The concept of actually being a slave is very difficult, if not actually repellent, for modern Christians, but perhaps contemporary Jewish custom offers an insight into Paul's thought.

In Jewish customary law, an adult son with his father had two choices. The son could take his inheritance in cash and make his own way in the world, though that was not usually regarded as wise. On the other hand, he could remain in his father's house, where he would then continue to be subject to his father's authority but could anticipate receiving his father's full inheritance in due course. The story of the Prodigal Son was one that Jesus' hearers would have recognised, however much they would have disapproved of the foolishness and greed of the younger son. What would have startled them was the willingness, indeed the eagerness, of this father to welcome this son home. Jesus leaves the story hanging in the air for everything thereafter

---

[16] Published in paperback by Arrow Books.
[17] John 15 v 15.
[18] See Galatians 4 v 1–7.

depended on individual human reaction: would the older in due course accept the younger? Would he provide for him after the father was gone? Would he share any part of the inheritance with him? Would he be vengeful, just or generous? We simply do not know.

The son who chose to stay at home was there voluntarily but, for so long as he chose to be there, he was under his father's authority. It was described as "being at the father's table" — which, of course, has rich symbolism for Christians who join together to celebrate the Eucharist. So for us: for so long as we choose to acknowledge ourselves as children of God, we are under his authority — it is a sort of slave-son picture. The key to it is that, in this life, we voluntarily accept the authority of the Father over every aspect of our lives whilst being, as adopted and beloved children, heirs to all that he has and intends to pour out on his children. Our internal security lies in our adoption.

I have often struggled with being — or rather feeling — a child of God. Being a servant, I can both understand and experience, but I have often regretted my apparent inability to feel the child of God. I, therefore, found this picture of the older brother who stayed at home both powerful and effective. As is often the case in the Christian life, we must live as God calls us to live and trust that the feelings will follow. Just as a good marriage essentially depends on an act of will (and trust that feelings will match that, at least from time to time!), so also the Christian life.

God, however, has a place for each of us in his world as his adopted child to be enjoyed as such through eternity. It is to that world, secure in our status that we must now turn.

CHAPTER 4

CALLED: OUR ROLE IN GOD'S WORLD

God has given us absolute security and status within his Kingdom by adopting us as his children. However, that is not something that is done just for its own sake but because God has a purpose for each one of us. On the night before he died, Jesus said to his disciples—

"You did not choose me, but I chose you and appointed you to go and bear fruit — fruit that will last."[19]

That is as true of us now as it was of them then. We are chosen and adopted but are then called to serve, to make available to God every fibre of our being.

The classic Christian word for this calling is *vocation,* but today it comes with difficulties. All too often, it has, to be blunt, been filched by the institutional church in order to recruit clergy or, perhaps more fairly, one should say, it is used by Christian groups to recruit people to what is described as "full-time Christian service/ministry". That generally means to service paid for by a Christian community. Now do not misunderstand me: of course, God calls people to ordination and other paid service within the Christian/church community. The problem is: what is heard by the ninety-five percent of Christians who are not so called? Does God have no call for us? Is our service part-time or

---

[19] John 15 v 16.

a bit part? Are we cameo Christians rather than those who have a major part? I want to argue that God calls every one of his adopted children and that he calls them all to full-time service in his world in which everything that happens is of concern and interest to him. We should therefore expect that he would call Christians to service in every aspect of his world.

That seems to me not only the necessary consequence of Jesus' words above but also the inevitable corollary of the Parable of the Talents.[20] All are called, all are equipped, and all are accountable. I understand that whilst much has been written about vocation in the narrow sense described above, very much less exists which considers this wider view. I have found some material produced either by academics or from within the church, but little or nothing written by those whose calling submerges them in our secular culture. Perhaps those with that insight have neither leisure nor inclination to write. Perhaps Western Christians are innately sceptical about the whole idea of God calling individuals. I do not claim to know the reason. I remember reading something by Os Guinness (but cannot now trace it) in which he directs us back to the work of the seventeenth-century Puritans who did understand this.

They contended that every Christian receives a double call from God: what they describe as a general vocation and a specific vocation. The first is a call common to all Christians: to become the people God intended us to be. The second is specific to each individual Christian: to a piece of service which you, as a unique child of God, can do as no other person quite could. A short reflection on each is called for.

The transformation from the person I am to the person that God created me to be is a lifelong quest that, in the Christian

---

[20] Matthew 25 v 14–30.

tradition I know best, is often called *sanctification*. It is the transforming work of the Holy Spirit at work within us by which the spoiling effect of sin on us yields to the emergence of the true person whom we were created to be. Much has been written about this, and I have no fresh light to shine on it, save to say that I have been deeply aware of the process at work within my own life. I would, however, like to offer a bit of context. To understand the true scope of this process, it needs to be seen in the light of one of the great principles that underpin all Christian understanding of God's work — *Shalom*.

Shalom is a Jewish concept encountered repeatedly in the Scriptures. It is traditionally translated as *peace,* but it has a much stronger meaning than its English equivalent. *Shalom* essentially concerns vibrant right relationships: between God and humanity, between people themselves and also between God, humanity and the created order. *Shalom* is the state in which all these mix, and relate in mutual harmony. It is the great overarching picture. We shall encounter it often enough in our thinking, but for now, we need to see it as the context within which each adopted child understands and works out their vocation to become the person they were created to be.

This process of transformation from who I am into whom I am intended to be is at the heart of our thinking about the call of God. It is the mindset that enables us to discern what specifically God would have us do. That is why our personal devotional life, the development of my relationship with God, is crucial to Christians living in this world. It is an aspect of that living that I have always found difficult and in which I have regularly needed the help of others. It is not a subject on which I feel qualified to contribute in any detail. I merely want to make the point that our relationship with God is critical to our service and repays all the effort that it requires.

All this has a further consequence. No Christian is ever entitled to compare themselves with another and certainly not in the quest for self-justification, which is why the Pharisee who looked down on the tax collector went home, as Jesus said, unjustified before God. [21] There is only one legitimate comparison open to the Christian: between myself as I am and myself as God would have me be. Paul put it like this:

"Each one should test his own actions. Then he can take pride in himself, without comparing himself to someone else, for each should carry his own load."[22]

When I give an account of my life, the spotlight will be on myself as I actually was compared to the person that God had created me to be.

That leads then to our specific vocation. Each of us is unique and is uniquely gifted. Each of us is called to a piece of service that, for that reason, no one else could quite do as we could. Each is called to a piece of service that will advance God's purposes for the created order. We may never in this life discern the true purpose of our life in the overall purposes of God, but in *Shalom*, it all fits together. I was directed to these words, attributed to Oscar Romero, by the late Bishop David Sheppard. It is, in fact, a prayer in memory of Oscar Romero. I find them helpful in enabling us to understand or accept our place in God's purposes.

"...The kingdom is not only beyond our efforts; it is beyond our vision. We accomplish in a lifetime only a fraction of the magnificent enterprise that is God's work... The kingdom always lies beyond us... [our work] may be incomplete, but it is a beginning, a step along the way, an opportunity for the Lord's

---

[21] Luke 18 v 9–14.
[22] Galatians 4 v 4–5.

41

grace to enter and do the rest. We may never see the end results, but that is the difference between the master builder and the workers. We are workers, not master builders."

We may never in this life discern the true purpose of our life in the overall purposes of God, but in *Shalom*, it all fits together. Sometimes I have found that frustrating, but of its truth, both in theology and practice, I have no doubt.

If God is the creator of the world and everything in it, then we should not be surprised that God calls his children to serve in each and every aspect of the created order. It may be in any area of life from the menial to the expert and whether paid or not.

As we reflect on this, it is crucial that we understand that God's call is to a service that is to be faithfully rendered. God's concern is faithfulness and not success. That is plain from the Parable of the Talents. Two servants were differently gifted but equally praised — "well done good and faithful servant". Our calling is to faithful service; its "success" is God's concern, not ours, for he alone knows his purposes. In a Western culture in which success is highly prized, it is all too easy for Christians to become discouraged, to think that they count for nothing or have nothing to offer. Irrespective of the gifts we have received, each of us is capable of faithful service. All of us need to remember Oscar Romero's perspective. All can live lives worthy of the accolade "well done, good and faithful servant". I must add that I have noticed in Matthew's account of this parable that the reward for the faithful discharge of responsibility is yet more responsibility. I have certainly found this to be so in my own life. This parable also offers a salutary warning, through the one with one talent, that no Christian can excuse inactivity by saying that he has nothing worth offering: every Christian is called and equipped for some service.

I do not want to pretend that any of this is easy. I always find it encouraging to read again the story of Moses' call.[23] You might have thought that a burning bush and the voice of God would be quite enough for Moses; not so. In fact, in what follows, there is much that is rich comedy. Each time God makes a point, Moses finds an excuse. He starts with — "who am I to do this?" I shall be with you, says God. "But who am I to say that you are?" God gives him an answer. "But suppose they don't listen to me?" God shows him how his staff will turn into a serpent: they will listen to him! "But I can't speak." Then Moses says (and how we can sympathize with him), "Oh, my Lord, please send someone else." God is not impressed, but patiently he offers Moses the services of his brother Aaron as a mouthpiece. Not perhaps a great start for Israel's greatest leader. The important thing, however, was that for all his doubts and fears, in the end, Moses obeyed and the rest, as they say, is history. We shall return to the centrality of obedience as a distinguishing mark of the Christian.

This specific vocation is not necessarily a once and for all experience. We may have parallel or serial vocations; some may be lifelong, while some may relate to a specific incident. We know almost nothing of a man called Hur save that on one occasion, he was instrumental in saving the army of the Jews by holding up the arms of Moses.[24] I want to fill out this idea of vocation from personal experience to show how it may work.

I consciously became a Christian shortly before my twelfth birthday, but it was at university that I began to think of what God was calling me to do. Not for me, fiery bushes or voices from God, I was left wrestling with the idea of being a barrister, teacher or vicar. I found myself in the Sudan doing twelve months as a

---

[23] Exodus 3 v1–4 v17.
[24] Exodus 17 v12.

43

teacher,[25] an experience that I thoroughly enjoyed but which showed me that a teaching career was not for me. This dawned early on in my time when after thirty hours on a train, I confronted a class of eighty-five teenage boys, most of whom seem to answer to the name of Mohammed. I thought it would be a good idea if I got them all to write their full names on a piece of paper, fold it over and put it on their desk so that I could learn them as I taught the lesson. The lesson went well and seemed to have been enjoyed by all. At break time, my rather serious head of department asked me how things had gone and what I had done. I told him. He looked at me and at the pieces of paper rather sorrowfully, telling me that those were not names but very naughty words!

I did however, whilst there, discover a call to the "inner city", as it was often described then, and was much influenced by Bruce Kendrick's book "Come out the Wilderness". I returned home and then accepted an offer in barristers' chambers in Liverpool. There I specialized (as I believed I was called to do) in those areas of law that most concern those at the bottom of the social pile: housing, childcare, domestic violence, crime, compensation and so forth. I had wanted to start a free legal advice centre but did not know where. I contacted someone whom I had known years before, who was then a curate in inner-city Liverpool. His team wanted a free legal advice centre but knew no one to run it. Thus did God confirm my calling.

I was greatly helped by other Christians, especially those who knew of life in the law or at least of its potential impact on others, leading me specifically to passages of Scripture that enabled me to get a much better understanding of the role of the advocate and judge in the purposes of God. The two most

---

[25] With Voluntary Service Overseas (VSO).

44

important were as follows:

"Speak out for those who cannot speak, for the rights of all the destitute. Speak out, judge righteously, defend the rights of the poor and needy."[26]

"He has told you, O mortal, what is good: and what does the Lord require of you but to do justice, and to love mercy (or kindness), and to walk humbly with your God?"[27]

I married Erica, and we ended up living in the area of the advice centre (and did so for another forty-six years), and in due course, we became parents and then local authority foster parents and then adopters. These were both serial and parallel vocations. They existed alongside a commitment to Christian hospitality at home and ministry as a Reader in our local church. There was also a call to work in our deprived community. My approach was to offer the professional services that few others could. Thus, I was happy to be secretary or treasurer of any group but chair of none. If we did not have a local person able and willing to chair, then as a community, we were not ready for that piece of work.

Furthermore, as an outsider to an area of Protestant/Catholic antipathy, we were able to offer the means by which practising Christians could worship and study together to show that that antipathy had no Christian basis to it. I had become secretary of our local community council and soon noticed that nearly everyone there was in church on Sunday but not in the same one. We were able to offer our home to allow Christians of all persuasions to meet and study and pray together. The local clergy encouraged us but initially thought they should not attend as they would inevitably be seen as standard-bearers. The group

---

[26] Proverbs 31 v 6–8.
[27] Micah 6 v 8: it is the motto verse of the Lawyers' Christian Fellowship.

flourished, and in due course, clergy did attend and participate. On one occasion, one of them asked when we were going to get onto things we disagreed over, to be met with the firm reply of a Roman Catholic layman: "But we haven't yet found anything that matters that we disagree about." That was a vivid lesson for us all: what matters when serving God and the world may not be quite the same as what matters in the Faculty of Theology. We were greatly assisted by the church culture in which we were working. Not only did we have supportive clergy, but there had been a recent ecumenical initiative known as Call to the North, and we were in the early period of the Bishop Sheppard and Archbishop Warlock partnership. Lasting fruit of these meetings is not only an annual ecumenical service on Good Friday (still well supported forty years on) but also, and crucially, an acceptance that working with people of other persuasions was entirely normal.

Meanwhile, I had finally come to accept that I was probably good for nothing except to be a barrister when a clergy friend, with whom I was discussing prospects of ordination, said that whilst I might make quite a good bishop, as a vicar, I would be a disaster. He was quite right then and probably still would be now — not quite like the great stories of Moses, Isaiah or Paul! That all led then to my becoming, in due time, a judge, first a circuit judge in Liverpool and then a High Court judge in London assigned to the Family Division. The old longings of being a teacher or vicar were, however, used, whether in ministry as a Reader or in my involvement in judicial education with what is now the Judicial College. God gives gifts individually as he pleases, but he uses them individually too — God's call is bespoke to each Christian. He does not give me the gifts to fulfil another's calling any more than he gifts another to fulfil mine —

there is no place for boasting or jealousy amongst the people of God. If a reminder be needed, Moses supplies it as he warns his people about preening themselves over their own prosperity:

"Do not say to yourselves, 'My power and the might of my own hand gained me this wealth.' But remember the Lord your God, for it is he who gives you the power to get wealth..."[28]

I regard every aspect of my life as an aspect of my call to full-time Christian service. I long that all other Christians might also see their lives as such and be encouraged by their Christian leaders so to do. There are areas of life outside the institutional church where discerning a Christian vocation may be easier. I am thinking of medicine, education, politics or social care. These tend to feature with some regularity in Sunday intercessions. My greater concern is for the rest of us — in finance, commerce, retail, transport, law or the "hospitality industry". Yet if we believe that God is interested in every aspect of life in his world, then we should expect him to call Christians into every aspect — whether prayed for on Sunday or not.

This is not the place for extensive autobiography beyond showing how the concept of God's call can work out in a life spent immersed in the secular institution of the law. It is my purpose, though, to assert that this was a Christian call, a call as profound and all-embracing as that of vicar, missionary, medical practitioner or teacher. As we have noted, humans were created as social, not solitary beings, and, given their propensity for going wrong, restraints were necessary. Law oiled by justice rather than naked force was God's provision. We should not be surprised that God calls some of his children to serve him there. All Christians should be able to identify and articulate what in God's world their own lives seek to advance and how in that

---

[28] Deuteronomy 8 v 17–18.

context, they can make a positive contribution to those who live in the world. That is the essence of understanding what Christian calling means. My call as a lawyer, or your call in administration, business, education, caring, cleaning or public transport — or indeed anywhere else — is as valid a vocation as a clergyperson in the sanctuary, a doctor in the surgery or a missionary in the field.

Even retirement does not put us beyond the call of God. He has a purpose for us throughout our life. So far as I can judge, the only retirement for a Christian occurs when carried out in a coffin. New fields await even at seventy or older, and so I have found. They may build on old skills (e.g., teaching) or may involve learning new ones — like trying to write a book! For many, retirement from regular employment brings opportunity to do things often longed for, and God may have a purpose behind it. No doubt as we grow older, the pressure and intensity of earlier life may lessen, but of work to be done — God's purposeful work — there seems to be plenty.

There is, however, a fundamental condition both to discerning God's call and to its implementation. That is obedience. Two passages of Scripture have struck me forcefully over the years. They do not make for comfortable reading not only because they are demanding but also because they expose us to risk and unpredictability.

First, when I read the "Farewell Discourses", recorded by John, spoken on the night before Jesus died, I am struck by Jesus' repeated association of love with obedience.

"If you love me, you will obey what I command"; "whoever has my commands and obeys them, he is the one who loves me"; "if anyone loves me, he will obey my teaching"; "if you obey my commands you will remain in my love"; "you are my friends if you do what I command you".[29]

Given that all this was spoken at a time when he knew that imminent death was certain, Jesus must have attached particular significance to it. It all ties in, of course, with the purpose of our adoption. We choose to accept his authority in our lives, and so he can call on us to advance his purposes in his world. Moses had put it succinctly to his people as they prepared to enter the promised land—

"So now, O Israel, what does the Lord your God require of you? Only to fear the Lord your God, to walk in all his ways, to love him, to serve the Lord your God with all your heart and with all your soul, and keep the commandments of the Lord your God and his decrees that I am commanding you today for your own well-being... Now what I am commanding you today is not too difficult for you or beyond your reach... No, the word is very near you, it is in your mouth and in your heart so that you may obey it."[30]

I am not convinced that we give this teaching today the weight it demands. Obedience is a distinctly unfashionable concept in modern Western thought, yet it seems to lie at the very heart of effective Christian living in that world. Christians need to rediscover the humility necessary to the practice of obedience.

If obedience is an unfashionable concept in our culture, then humility is almost unfathomable. In a culture that emphasizes the individual, it is the achievements, rights and entitlements of the individual that take centre stage. Humility (and its more common word *modesty*) actually seeks both to put the individual in a different context and to emphasise the individuality of others. Thus, the humble person neither exalts nor abases himself. He

---

[29] John 14 v15, 21, 23; 15 v10, 14.
[30] Deuteronomy 10 v 12–15; 30 v 11–14.

compares himself not with others but with himself as God would want him to be. The humble person, in consequence, pours a healthy dose of cold water on his pride. On the other hand, the humble person knows that he is uniquely valued by God and adopted into his family, and you cannot say better than that. The humble person, in consequence, pours a healthy dose of cold water on all those self-doubts about worth, significance and purpose. Paul offers a powerful example of the practice of humility when he writes to his friends in Rome—

"For by the grace given to me, I say to everyone among you not to think of yourselves more highly than you ought to think, but to think with sober judgment, each according to the measure of faith that God has assigned."[31]

Obedience and humility are closely linked for a Christian. It is when I know how far short of God I fall, that I know the need to follow Maker's Instructions. It is when I know how valued I am by God that I long to please him by doing as he asks. It is when I know that I am part of the created order that I want to see other people valued as I know myself to be. The humble person truly understands the second great commandment. A meditation not only on the Cross but also on why Jesus had to die is, as many have pointed out, no bad place to start in the quest for Christian humility.

The second passage of Scripture is to be found in the call of Isaiah,[32] and that offers a further insight. The prophet has a dramatic encounter with God, but it is the sequel that is important here. God says, "Whom shall I send, and who will go for us?" To which Isaiah replies, "Here am I. Send me." It is then that God gives him his appointed task. The sequence here is important.

---

[31] Romans 12 v 3.
[32] Isaiah 6 v 1–8 especially v 8.

God calls, Isaiah responds, and then the content of the call is revealed. What matters here is Isaiah's obedient heart. For him, it is enough that God calls.

Discovering our calling can be hard, especially for Western Christians. God does not play hide and seek with us, but we do not seem to share the experience of other Christians (especially outside the West) of encountering God through dreams or even hearing his voice or being visited by an angel. God seems to have to approach his modern Western children (or this one at least) rather more cerebrally. Some Christians who find it hard to discern God's call may, however, have got the sequence the wrong way round. They want God to reveal the content before they respond. God, however, does not do deals; he does not offer us the choice to accept or decline as though our call was a job offer. God's call is to a life of obedient service and, when that has been responded to, then God reveals to the obedient spirit what is required. This can be quite scary.

Obedience does not come naturally to Western humanity. An individualistic secular culture rebels against any such concept. It is particularly difficult for those (and they include me) who exercise authority and leadership in our lives. Yet it is an inescapable Christian teaching, the essence of which is an obedient spirit. And this is something essentially cultivated in the process of sanctification that we thought about before. It is something of particular need to those who exercise authority and power. The Christian judge, government official or teacher needs to exercise authority and power founded in an obedient spirit, accepting that all they do is not only part of our God-given vocation but is also something for which we will be held personally accountable before God. How good it is that we serve a God who is slow to anger and of great kindness.

God reveals his purpose for us to the extent that we need to know and are capable of understanding it. He also reveals it when we need to know it and not when we would like to know. This can be uncomfortable and disconcerting. We have forgotten as a society how to wait. The old credit card adage that the card takes the waiting out of wanting has deeply penetrated our culture. Waiting is countercultural and frustrating but waiting is also a necessary skill for those who serve God, for God's timescales are not ours.

"Be still before the Lord, and wait patiently for him; do not fret over those who prosper in their way."[33]

Adoption is, however, a permanent relationship of which service is an integral part but not the whole. We are not God's contractors but his children. Thus, the scariness, the riskiness and the unpredictability have to be seen in the context of our unshakeable security as the adopted children of God.

As Christian people, we need to recover and re-assert God's vocation for everyone. It may find many expressions, but all will have in common service within God's world. No vocation is more important than another, for each has its unique part to play in the working out of God's purposes. We should respect and value every Christian's vocation as we do our own. Each of us is called to faithful service, and thus each of us is called to live and work to the same standard and the same quality. What is important is that we nurture obedient spirits that are open to respond to God's choice of service for us in his world and to respond with faithfulness in accordance with his choice.

---

[33] Psalm 37 v 7.

CHAPTER 5

WORKERS: PICTURES OF CHRISTIAN LIVING

Christians are chosen and called by God so that they may live and work effectively in the service of the Kingdom. There are two questions that arise. The first relates to the extent of the kingdom; in other words, is this all about service within the church and amongst the people of God or is it wider than that, and, if so, what is it? Secondly, it concerns the whole idea of how we live and serve being dictated by the nature of the society that we live in. To talk of living and serving in a rural agrarian economy, in which many people rarely moved from the place where they were born, is quite different to a highly mobile urban community where it is entirely realistic to talk of the global village. How then does teaching framed in one context (for example, the teachings of Jesus and the Scriptures) make sense in one that would not have been within their human contemplation? Those of us who remember the UK in the middle of the twentieth century sometimes have to pinch ourselves as we remember the huge cultural changes that have taken place in our lifetime. My grandchildren may find my accounts of my childhood as different to theirs as theirs is to those they learn about in history lessons.

Our first question takes us back to our understanding of the created order. If it be true that the earth is the Lord's because through him it was created, then our context for Christian living and service must surely embrace the whole created order. Of course, there will be those whose work is focused on the church and the people of God, but the whole context for service is the whole of creation. Although at present, acknowledgment of the authority of God and the Kingdom is a voluntary act by those chosen and called as God's children, it is at the heart of the Christian faith that in the end, the Kingdom of God and his Authority will be declared over the whole world and the whole of the created order. It follows that Christians should be studying and seeking to understand the teachings of their Faith in that wide context. We should be expecting to live, work and serve in every aspect of creation, whether or not those around us acknowledge the authority of our God and whether or not those present aspects formed any part of the understanding of the original teacher.

It follows then that we will have to hear, understand and seek to apply the teachings of the Faith in a context radically different from that in which they were first propounded. If the purpose of the teachings of prophets, Messiah and apostles was to enable the people of God to live as such in the place where God had put them, then we should expect those teachings to be rooted in the culture and time in which they were delivered. At the same time, we need to acknowledge that these teachings have universal application in the sense that the principles of life, work and service of the People of God in their place in the created order would apply irrespective of the context of culture and time in which they were being explored. Our task is, of course, first to understand how these teachings were perceived by their first hearers or readers, then to distil the essential principles that underpin that teaching before then seeking to understand and apply those principles in our own time and culture.

Many books have been written about this, and everyone who reflects on this process must necessarily be either highly selective or go on forever. There may be a sense of relief in my recognition that I shall have to be highly selective, but I want at this stage to concentrate on something specific. In his teachings, Jesus uses three pictures or metaphors of Christian living: salt, light and yeast. In one sense, those pictures are limited by culture, but in another, they are capable of living independently of culture and thus to be of universal application. At the same time, we have to recognise that our understanding of these pictures or metaphors is also constrained by our own culture. We have a lesser regard for salt than did first-century Israel, but we have a much more complex understanding of light. However, provided we can appreciate the cultural implications for both teacher and disciple, these pictures or metaphors may still be very fruitful. I want to start with salt.

SALT
Salt was a crucial and valuable substance in the ancient world with, as we shall see, key properties that made it a fundamental constituent of life. It plays a different role today, for much of its use is within commercial processes and thus outside our immediate observation. Indeed, it has acquired a bit of a reputation as a danger to health mainly through its overuse in those processes. Culturally it is perceived quite differently in our world to how it was seen in the ancient world. That said, many connections remain — we still value it as a condiment just as we still do recognise former salt mines as ideal places to store valuable things that would be damaged by a damp atmosphere. There were many treasures evacuated from London during the Second World War that were stored in the salt mines of Cheshire,

for example. If, however, we are to understand Jesus' teaching that "you are the salt of the earth",[34] we shall only do it full justice when we recognise how his hearers would have perceived salt. We need, therefore, to grasp the perceived qualities of salt as understood by the hearers of Jesus if we are to give full weight to the metaphor as we try to apply it to our own lives.

Salt was and has always been a flavourer of food. Just as food is enhanced by a little salt, so should our community be enhanced by the presence of the people of God. It should simply be a better place because of their presence. Paul put it like this to his friends at Colossae:

"Let your speech always be gracious, seasoned with salt, so that you may know how you ought to answer everyone."[35]

What should be true of our speech should be true of every part of our life. This is not to define salt, simply to describe its function. I have been increasingly impressed by the importance of Christian witness through mere presence; whether it is in the place we call home or where we work. The very fact of our presence opens channels of blessing to others.

A striking example of that is found in the story of Abraham. God decides to reveal to Abraham his intention to destroy Sodom and Gomorrah as his judgment against them. Abraham's response is bold:

"Will you indeed sweep away the righteous with the wicked? Suppose there are fifty righteous within the city; will you then sweep away the place and not forgive it for the fifty righteous who are in it. Far be it from you to do such a thing... Shall not the Judge of the earth do what is just?"

And what was God's response?

---

[34] Matthew 5 v 13.
[35] Colossians 4 v 6.

"If I find at Sodom fifty righteous in the city, I will forgive the whole place for their sake." Emboldened, Abraham tries his luck with forty and gets the same response. Thirty? Twenty? Ten? "For the sake of ten, I will not destroy it." Sadly, none were found, and the cities were destroyed.[36] Suppose, however, that there had been ten such; what blessing and mercy their mere presence would have ensured. When we wait patiently for God, our apparent inactivity may be much more fruitful than we ever imagined it could be.

In Jeremiah (and we will look at the specific passage shortly), we find God offering prosperity to Babylon simply because his people were there. I am not advocating inaction, but I am advocating a willingness to be where God would bless and to be the means by which he does just that. Salt seasons simply through its presence in something, invisible though its activity may be. It is an important message when facing discouragement because nothing seems to have happened.

Perhaps more important in the ancient world, and indeed in the whole world prior to our understanding of refrigeration, was salt's function as a preservative. If you have food, meat, for example, that was liable to go off, rot and become useless, you needed to preserve it. Salt performed that function. Salt's usefulness was effectively in direct proportion to the capacity of the specific food to rot. That seems to me a particularly powerful aspect of the metaphor or picture of Christians as the salt of the earth. It means surely that we should expect God to place (and thus for the church to find) Christians in all sorts of religiously unpromising places in society. Indeed, the worse that aspect of society is likely to be, arguably the more we should expect to find that God has placed Christians there as preservatives. Is that, in

---

[36] Genesis 18 v 16–33 and 19.

fact, how we in the church today actually see things?

I had Christian colleagues in the law who refused to practise in family law. For some, it was because they did not see themselves as temperamentally suited to the work, and we should respect that. It is a fundamental precept amongst the judiciary that all family judges should be volunteers. To have any chance of doing the work effectively, they must want to do it. Many colleagues, however, had not got that far. They refused because they thought the work to be ethically dubious, involving pandering to human sinfulness. I can see what they mean. Yet not only are humans often in the deepest pain when involved in child abuse and relationship breakdown, but humanity is also encountered at its most corruptible. Surely in those circumstances being the salt of the earth means deep involvement where there is hurt and a potential for corruption, whatever the risks may be.

You can replicate that idea, of course, across the whole breadth of human experience; I choose this one because it is my experience. Farmers must grow food and make a living just as they must protect the environment. Business executives must turn a profit, produce a worthwhile product and have regard for those who work for them. Financial managers have clients who wish to make money, but their actions may have much wider consequences. Whatever we do, there will be tensions for Christians to confront and not to avoid.

There are two short passages in the Bible that seem to me vivid examples of this. The first is the letter of Jeremiah to the exiles in Babylon.[37] Here are Jews exiled to the land of bitter enemies who have desecrated and destroyed the Temple, Jews crushed by the apparent severity of God's judgment. And the

---

[37] Jeremiah 29.

message: live life to the full and —

"Seek the welfare of the city where I have sent you into exile, and pray to the Lord on its behalf, for in its welfare you will find your welfare... For surely I know the plans I have for you, says the Lord, plans for your welfare and not for harm, to give you a future with hope."[38]

Here was God placing his people in the heart of pain and corruption and urging them to seek the best for all those around. That, for me, is a classic model of being the salt of the earth. I may not like where I am, I may not like the culture in which I find myself, but this is God's creation, loved by him, and I am to be a flavourer and a preservative within it.

The second is to be found towards the end of the Book of Revelation. The writer is observing and describing the fall of Babylon, where Babylon represents the aggregate of human arrogance, power and sinfulness. Then, just as the judgment is about to fall, he hears these words: "Come out of her, my people..."[39] Now I am wary of too close analysis of apocalyptic writing, but it has always seemed to me to confirm that the people of God are to be found in all human activity, flavouring and preserving the unattractive and the corruptible, until nothing further is to be done before God sets all creation to rights.

The idea of being a preservative is, of course, deeply risky; contamination is a perennial danger. We may remember the seed in the Parable of the Sower that was choked by the cares of the world — a real enough issue in the world in which we live. However, the fact that it is risky and potentially dangerous is not a justification for avoiding it. I believe that the whole metaphor of salt is predicated on such a risk: how could it be otherwise?

---

[38] v 7, 11.
[39] Revelation 18 v 4.

Contamination is a real danger, not least because we are often exposed to spiritual as well as human forces. Paul writes:

"For our struggle is not against flesh and blood but against the rulers, against the authorities, against the powers of this dark world and against the spiritual forces of evil in the heavenly realms."[40]

In doing so, he identifies the true sources of contamination.

We should squarely face the risks and dangers of contamination. We will all know Christians who have plunged into areas of business, manufacture, law, finance or other fields of work and whose involvement seems to have sucked their faith out of them. Very often, this happens surreptitiously so that the person concerned is not aware of what is happening until it is often too late. That is, of course, one reason why we need to be in touch with other Christians in our area of work or life. It is also why we need to be vigilant to hear God's call and why every Christian should be encouraged to do so. If we are not where God wants us to be, then we may not be equipped to resist contamination. To follow a respectable job simply to enable us to be involved heavily in the life of the church may be right if a Christian has been specifically so-called (e.g., a self-supporting minister) but otherwise not only will it limit their contribution where they work, it may also leave them unknowingly exposed to contamination. In this area, we need to be vigilant and to ensure that we have access to the necessary resources, as we shall consider later in chapter 8.

If I were to serve you a succulent steak and then spread on it an equivalent weight of salt, you would not thank me; indeed, the food would in practice be inedible. It is of the essence of salt that it is always a minority and a tiny minority at that. A few crystals

---

[40] Ephesians 6 v 12.

will usually suffice. So it is with Christians within the created order. We should never be surprised, indeed we should expect, to find ourselves to be a small minority. That is how the salt of the earth works. The Jews were a tiny and insignificant minority in Babylon, yet God had a profound purpose for them. It is no different today. Wherever God has placed us in community or work as his people, we should expect to be in a minority. Of course, some of us will exercise secular authority, but salt does not do its work by domination but by a gradual seeping into every part of the substance it has been put into. The work of salt is not a blitz on the citadel of secularism but a quiet, faithful working alongside others within that citadel; this change comes from within.

Salt also involves sociability. Salt on its own is useless; its usefulness depends upon its reaction with something else, whether food or a slippery road. But for Jesus' hearers, salt was a sign of hospitality, you shared salt with your guest, a concept that has continued into our culture and indeed our language: "eating my salt" means receiving my hospitality (although now a rather quaint metaphor). The salt of the earth is only effective as such when in relation with other humans or communities, or institutions. That is how it works. I have become increasingly aware over the years of the emphasis in the New Testament on hospitality, in particular on the use of our homes in the service of God. It is a matter to which we must return.

I should, in fairness, add a warning note. Salt can also be an irritant. That may be healthy in the sense that it prevents us from ingesting too much, but it does also just happen because salt is salt. We should not be surprised if some around us are uncomfortable with our presence. That may have the good effect of preventing us from being unduly forceful, but it may also be that salt is simply salt that has retained its saltiness. Some discomfort or even opposition is not an uncommon experience when salt is acting as salt should. The teachings of Jesus are full of warnings that his followers might not enjoy universal popularity. The man in Nelson's Navy who had been flogged then had salt rubbed into his wounds. This was not to prolong his agony (though, of course, it would do so) but to prevent his wounds from becoming infected. In those days, an operation at sea was much safer than in hospital since at sea, there was a much greater control of infection. The irritant may be beneficial.

There is, however, one further aspect of salt that would have been familiar enough to Jesus' hearers but would not resonate with the modern reader. Salt was an integral part of the Jewish sacrificial system. So, in the description of this system in Leviticus, we read:

"...You shall not omit from your grain offerings the salt of the covenant with your God: with all your offerings, you shall offer salt."[41]

The salt of the earth is, therefore, intimately connected with the religious life.

Many theologians over history have sought to elicit meaning from this. For me, it is a reminder that to be effective salt of the earth, we need always to remain as a member of the worshipping community. However deeply involved we may be in however distant a part of the created order, we need each other. To his words that we are the salt of the earth, Jesus added these —

"... But if salt has lost its taste, how can its saltiness be restored? It is no longer good for anything but is thrown out and trampled underfoot."[42]

---

[41] Leviticus 2 v 13.
[42] Matthew 5 v 13.

The worshipping community and the resources available to a Christian (considered later) are the means by which saltiness is retained and refreshed. Our call to isolated service in risky areas makes active church membership more, not less, important. Bishop Stuart Blanch of Liverpool was once asked whether it was possible to be a Christian but not go to church. He said that it was but that he had never met such a person — overstated no doubt but with more than a grain of truth to it.

Salt was an essential in the world of Jesus' earthly life. The salt of the earth remains an essential in God's world of today, and all of us are to serve in that role. We are chosen and called to make the world a better place by our presence, to act as a preservative wherever rot threatens and to recognise that we will usually be in a minority. Yet to be effective, we must be in relation with all around us whilst at the same time remaining an active member of a worshipping community.

Certainly, salt was not the only metaphor Jesus used and, therefore, not the only one that we should consider. For me, it has been powerful and helpful, no doubt, because I have found it highly relevant to the issues which have been most important to me. I fully recognise that others may have differing views as to which metaphor is the most helpful.

LIGHT

So what about light? Jesus' words after salt continue as follows:

"You are the light of the world. A city built on a hill cannot be hidden. No one, after lighting a lamp, puts it under the bushel basket, but on a lampstand, and it gives light to all in the house. In the same way, let your light shine before others so that they may see your good works and give glory to your Father in heaven."[43]

Whilst the work of salt is often unseen, there is no mistaking a light. Just as we are not to advertise ourselves in the work to which we are called, so we are to take no steps to hide ourselves. We are to be what we are, however public or private our role may actually cause us to be. As we have seen, humility does not seek the limelight, but neither does it cower in the shadows. It does what needs to be done wherever that might be, however public or private, and does it faithfully to honour Our Lord.

There has been so much written about the Christian as the light of the world that I am wary of trying to add anything to it, but perhaps I can make three points that have emerged from my experience. The first is that we only need light where otherwise there would be darkness. Thus, we are again reminded that Christians are needed in the darkest parts of life, and we should not be surprised to find them, or indeed ourselves, there. Of course, just as salt can be an irritant, so light is not always welcome in dark places.

Secondly, light can be seen from a much greater distance than can actually be seen by the light itself. You will have stood on a hillside at night and watched car headlights in the distance pointing away from you: they cannot see you, but you can see them. Or think again of navigation lights in a river. The red and green lights illuminate little around them, but they can be seen at a distance, and they are essential to finding safe passage up the river or into port. Our lives may not illuminate what is around us, but they will certainly be seen by very many others and may have an effect on the basis of pointing the way to others.

And that brings us to the third point: we will never know this side of death the effect that our life may have had on others for

---

[43] Matthew 5 v 14–16.

good or ill. Others may see and react to or be affected by our lives without us having any inkling of it. That is why the Christian call is to faithful service. The lights must be in the right place in the channel: it is the responsibility of others as to what they choose to make of them. We are to do everything that needs to be done not because it advertises God (or ourselves) but simply because it is right to do it whether anyone else knows of it or not. It is a case of the left hand not necessarily needing to know what the right hand is doing.

YEAST

Jesus uses yeast as a picture of the Kingdom of God.

"The kingdom of heaven is like yeast that a woman took and mixed in with three measures of flour until all of it was leavened."[44]

It describes in part the place of the Christian in the created order serving as the leaven. It can be used to reinforce points already made, and I would only want to make one further point. God is the baker; he chooses where and how the yeast is mixed, and he, and he alone, decides when all of it is leavened. Again, this is a reminder not only of a call to faithful service but also a call to trusting service. As the words attributed to Oscar Romero remind us, we are unlikely to know this side of death what part we have played in the purposes of God. But we do know this: that faithful service does play a part in those purposes and, without that service, those purposes are not fulfilled quite as God would have wanted.

All this talk of our service has nothing to do with worldly status, natural talent or education but everything to do with our faithful obedience to what God has called us. No doubt God has

---

[44] Matthew 13 v 33.

a place for the learned; no doubt he has a place for those who exercise authority (after all, we believe that this authority derives from him); no doubt he has a place for the highly talented (after all, we believe that these are gifts from him). However, none of that is relevant to whether we deliver for God the life of faithful obedience that he seeks from every one of us. If confirmation of this be needed, we should look again at these words of Paul —

"Consider your own call, brothers and sisters: not many of you were wise by human standards, not many were powerful, not many were of noble birth. But God chose what is foolish in the world to shame the wise; God chose what is weak in the world to shame the strong; God chose what is low and despised in the world, things that are not, to reduce to nothing things that are, so that no one might boast in the presence of God."[45]

I am not sure that the Western Church, with its highly professional leadership, has ever quite believed this, but it remains nevertheless true.

I have chosen to reflect on these three pictures or metaphors because they are employed by Jesus as metaphors for living as the People of God in God's world and because they have helped me as I have tried faithfully to follow the service entrusted to me. They are, however, metaphors and not allegories, so we need to take care how far they are pressed. What they do, however, is to tell us that the normal Christian life will involve working as a small minority in some of the most secular aspects of our culture and that we have been chosen and called along that road as part of the working out of God's great work of salvation of the world he created and which he loves.

---

[45] I Corinthians 1 v 26–29.

CHAPTER 6

WORKERS: MODELS FOR CHRISTIAN LIVING

The world of first-century Palestine was unrecognizably different to that of the twenty-first-century Western world today. Any reading across from one to the other requires great care; in particular, we have to guard against reading the unspoken assumptions of our culture (which may be so deeply etched in us that we are not even aware of them) into the teachings of the Bible. At the same time, the human condition has not changed much; we can visualise the personalities of the Bible with all their strengths and, yes, all their faults too. So teaching as to the human condition can transfer more easily across the centuries. The central core of humanity — us — is largely unchanged. It is the context in which we live where change has been so profound. Thus, the pictures or metaphors offered of salt, light and yeast can speak directly to us as humans; it is seeing how they work in the context of the modern world that causes the difficulty.

I have developed an understanding of how these things might work in the area of the law. However, the Bible has much to say about money and business integrity. It has much to say about an employer's treatment of employees. One of the great tirades that the prophets deliver time and again concerns, as we have seen, the use of false weights in trade. The Jewish law made provision for it, and, of course, Jesus had more to say about money than he ever did about sex.

However, as well as pictures or metaphors, the Bible offers us some models of Christian living by identifying certain human roles which can illuminate how the life of faith can be lived with integrity today. Again, we must be cautious about context. However, the models offered do resonate in the modern world — we are familiar with them. I have chosen three: the ambassador, the steward and the tenant. I want to suggest that reflection on each may shed light on our task as God's chosen and called workers. Again, this is not an exhaustive list, and others may have found and chosen other models. These three have been important for me, and I believe can be helpful for others too.

AMBASSADOR

I want to start with the ambassador, if only because it is a model that has had a profound impact on my life. It is not that I know many ambassadors or a great deal about the diplomatic life. Indeed, my only real experience was in Khartoum in 1969–70, a year I spent as a volunteer teacher in the Northern Sudan. It did, however, make quite an impression. The embassy staff, who seemed very welcoming to us, were very much committed to being active friends to the Sudanese, and most were fluent in Arabic. At the same time, the culture of the embassy was unashamedly British, down to afternoon tea at four p.m. and bacon for breakfast. They were involved and yet were also distinctive.

The ambassador himself was there both representing the British government, whose relations with the Sudanese government even then were not always easy, and as the personal representative of the Sovereign. His role was to balance the desire to be a friend to the Sudanese people, the requirement to advance the interests of his government and his obligation to represent the person of the Queen.

Paul talks of the ambassador of Christ specifically in two places,[46] and there are allusions to the concept elsewhere in the New Testament. As I have reflected on this, I have seen what to me has been a compelling model for Christian living and service. The key is the paradox of being involved and yet distinctive.[47]

The teachings of Jesus abound in paradox. Whoever loves his life will lose it, and whoever loses his life will save it; whoever gives up everything for him will find true riches; and indeed, you cannot understand the Transfiguration without the Cross and vice versa. You can see it in Paul as well as in the passage we looked at in the last chapter of the foolish confounding the wise.[48] This paradox of being involved yet distinctive fits a New Testament pattern.

Once again, we are reminded that in a world all of which belongs to God, we should expect to find Christians anywhere and everywhere. Our country has embassies in lands both friendly and unfriendly. Indeed, it is often particularly important to have skilled diplomats and representatives in unfriendly places. The more difficult the culture, the more adaptable the ambassador must be. The embassies in Washington, Brussels and Beijing will be very important, but so are those in Khartoum, Pyongyang or Damascus. All in their way are significant, but the working out of the role will be very different in each place. It follows that we should expect God to send his ambassadors to every corner of human life, and we should be ready for him to

---

[46] II Corinthians 5 v 20 and Ephesians 6 v 20.
[47] Again I owe the roots of this thinking to Roger Dowley.
[48] I Corinthians 1 v 26.

send some of the most gifted to some of the least friendly and promising destinations.

I found myself spending a working life in the law and, in particular, in family and related law. The law, although having demanding ethical standards, prides itself on being a highly secularized profession. Judges serve as "secular judges" administering civil or "secular" law. They are set apart from religious and political traditions and systems. In that sense (as well as in the separation of powers), they are independent. A Christian called to be a lawyer or judge necessarily finds himself in that culture and necessarily discovers, like the ambassador to Khartoum or Pyongyang, that the prevailing culture and language are very different to that in which he had been brought up. Yet the call is to become involved.

It would be presumptuous of me to tell others what becoming involved might mean. Certainly, for me, it was engagement with the hurt and pain of others and with the protection of those least able to protect themselves in a crisis. It did not mean abandoning Christian principles, but it did mean allowing to others their God-given rights and responsibilities of choice and decision. I may not have been at ease with the life choices made by others, but that was their responsibility, and they would be held accountable for it. I discuss this more in the next chapter.

However, one task was that of language. The language of the law is carefully framed in secular terms, and very much uses human rights to underpin it ethically. None of that is necessarily inconsistent with Christian values. As has been observed, the concept of human rights has its origins in the thinking of John Locke, the seventeenth-century English philosopher, who based it on the proposition in Genesis that humanity is created in the

70

image of God and therefore necessarily acquires certain rights that govern the relationship between human beings and in particular between human beings and the state. You do not hear these origins often acknowledged today.

One of the tasks of the ambassador is to frame Christian values in the language of the current culture; thus, when considering in legal proceedings whether to withdraw treatment from a baby with no real hope of independent survival, a decision has to be justified in the language of the welfare of the child as the paramount consideration; that is the statutory requirement. A decision authorizing withdrawal of treatment based on that approach may sound different to the language of the moral theologian, but the substance is, and should be, essentially the same. It might be helpful to give a specific example, and so I have taken part of a judgment of my own in such a case. It was the case in which a child suffered a catastrophic injury and was being kept alive by the technical skills of the intensive care unit staff. However, they had concluded that all treatment was now futile and even painful for the child and should be withdrawn. The parents disagreed; for them whilst there was life there was hope and they had religious reasons for their disagreement. The dispute could not be resolved and so it came to court before me.

"The next task is to address the issue of X's welfare. That assessment must be the court's independent assessment, but it must be one that looks at all relevant issues from the assumed point of view of the patient; a necessary but artificial exercise in some ways it may be thought. Yet it is rightly so required, for X is a human being of unique value: body, mind and spirit expressed in the unique personality that is X. It is important that 'quality-of-life' judgments are not made through other eyes, for 'quality-of-life' may weigh very differently with different people depending on their individual views and aspirations. A life from which others may recoil can yet be precious [to the one who lives it]. At the same time, preservation of life, however important, cannot be everything. No understanding of life is complete unless it has in it a place for death, which comes to each and every human with unfailing inevitability. There is unsurprisingly deep in the human psyche, a yearning that, when the end comes, it does so as a 'good death'. It is often easier to say what that is not rather than what it is, but in this case, the contrast is between a death in the arms and presence of parents and a death wired up to machinery and so isolated from all human contact in the course of futile treatment."[49]

In the end, I decided that the treatment should be withdrawn and the baby be allowed to die. What I said can be found in no Act of Parliament, appellate court decision or legal textbook. It is simply an attempt to articulate welfare in a particular case; an attempt to cast Christian values in secular language.

How then do we see the role of the Christian ambassador serving in highly secularized cultures? I want to suggest three aspects that may help so far as being involved is concerned. No doubt there are many others, but these three have certainly kept me fully occupied.

First, do what you do as well as you can do it. We are where God has put us to do whatever it may be. At the heart of our witness is a commitment to do what he has given us to do as well as we can do it. I remember being on a course with two Christian engineers who worked in the field of heavy vehicles. I was struck by their complaint about Christian colleagues who did just what they had to do, and no more, at work so they could give their time to church-based work. I have no doubt that those colleagues were

---

[49] NHS TRUST V BABY X [2012] EWHC 2188 (Fam) at paras 24,25.

commended by their church for the time that they gave. Indeed, they were probably heeding an unspoken but clearly implied message from their pulpit that real Christian work is what you do under the banner of the church. Yet these two other Christians lamented the effect on their witness at work. Had their colleagues seen, or been taught or encouraged to see, that God wants ambassadors who are necessarily working away from formal church activity? To do the job as well as you can is a key witness of the ambassador. I may or may not have been a "successful" barrister or judge, but I did seek to be the best that I could be in the work that I had been given to do.

Sometimes Christians find real guidance in the Bible for the job that they have. I have already mentioned two passages,[50] but I have also found real help in the charge given by King Jehoshaphat, after his reforms, to his judges:

"Consider what you are doing, for you judge not on behalf of human beings but on the Lord's behalf; he is with you in giving judgment. Now, let the fear of the Lord be upon you; take care what you do, for there is no perversion of justice with the Lord our God, or partiality, or taking of bribes."[51]

As I have already said, I have been surprised as I have discovered how great an emphasis there is on justice in the Bible and the strength of the language that is so often used when confronting injustice.

Those who work in commerce or housing or in the armed services or in government will also find specific teaching that they can apply to their daily lives. Indeed, whatever we are called to do, whether paid or unpaid, is open to guidance from the principles that we can discover in the Bible. To make those

---

[50] Proverbs 31 v 6–8 and Micah 6 v 8.
[51] II Chronicles 19 v 6–7.

discoveries, our primary resource is likely to be Christians who have already trodden that way.

However, most of us working in secular cultures will have to work out for ourselves what it is that we are to do. How we are to equip ourselves and how to do that are things we will think about in a later chapter. The key principle is, however, very simple: as the personal representatives of the Sovereign, we do what he has called us to do as well as we are able to do it.

The second facet of involvement as an ambassador is engagement with the ethical issues of the area in which we serve. This is essential for two reasons. First, others will expect us as Christians to have views and will actually want to know what they are. If we disappoint them here, why should they listen to us speaking about things that we think they should see as important, like the challenge of the gospel? Secondly, ethical thinking is difficult for the secularist because of the difficulty of finding an agreed starting point in an ethical discussion, and such a discussion is very difficult if there is no agreed starting point. I remember watching a TV programme about the storing of frozen embryos. The distinguished panel of clinicians, lawyers, ethicists and theologians could all agree that significant ethical issues were involved and that those issues would both require regulation and inform the ambit of it, but they were unable to find an agreed starting point for their discussion. Christians can often make an important and necessary contribution in these ethical issues.

Now I am not talking about those issues over which Christians have always held strong views like the pictures on the calendars in the cafeteria (important though that may be) but issues that lie at the heart of our work: why do we do it? Who is affected by it? Does it tend to the common good? How are the fruits of our labours shared? How do we balance profit against

74

safety and quality? And so on. So as a judge, I tried to engage with the ethics of power as well as justice and, in particular, with the vast discretionary powers given to trial judges in the Family Court and the Court of Protection. I have written on this, trying at the same time both to honour Christian values and yet express them in language that the intended reader can access and understand. [52] No doubt, our opportunities to do this will be different depending on what we do and our experience within that. However, it is something that we all can and should do as opportunity offers.

In truth, it is difficult to overstate the importance of engagement with ethical issues, whether in the workplace or in community involvement. Anyone working in healthcare knows the tension between targets and good treatment, just as every teacher knows it between exam results and good learning. Every farmer knows the tension between productivity and the care of the environment, just as every driver knows that between speed and safety. How many others encounter conflict between profits and service or quality? How many of us are tempted to flirt with communication that diverts from the truth or manipulates? Many of these can be quite subtle but nonetheless uncomfortable. There are, of course, the more overt issues like fraud or abuse of power, bullying or sexual harassment. Though these can be seen in others and should not be allowed to pass unchallenged, they are less obvious to us when in us. When does risk-taking become an abuse of power, or the firm exercise of authority become bullying? We can be very adept at concealing these things from ourselves. However, God is not misled: "O Lord, you have searched me and known me... You discern my thoughts from far

---

[52] The Modern Judge published 2016 by LexisNexis.

away."[53] No wonder the Psalmist says elsewhere: "but who can detect their errors? Clear me from hidden faults."[54]

The third area relates to evangelism. I am not alone amongst Christians in finding this difficult. Many of us will have encountered the heavy-handed approach, especially in the workplace, that has the effect too often of repelling rather than attracting. There is something slightly uncomfortable in using the semi-captive element of a workplace audience to preach, especially if one is in a position of authority or power. At the same time, complete silence is a betrayal of our call as Christians and is undermining of our sense of vocation in being where we are. I think that the model of the ambassador offers three clues that may be helpful.

First, it is his responsibility to ensure that the government of the country where he serves understands the policies of his government. This is a further reason why engagement in ethical discussion is essential. You are being asked as a Christian, and you may properly reply as such. Secondly, his own life and personality should reflect that of the Sovereign, and we will look further at this when we come to the distinctiveness of the ambassador. It is said that St Francis of Assisi said to his brothers: "Go and preach the gospel and use words where necessary." How we live often counts for more than what we say, and it is doubly damaging if what we say is, in fact, denied by how we live. What we have already seen in the writings of Isaiah and Amos should serve as powerful warnings for us today.

Thirdly, the ambassador will always speak of his country and its values when asked to do so. I have always found help in these words of Peter:

---

[53] Psalm 139 v 1–2.
[54] Psalm 19 v 12.

"Always be ready to make your defence to anyone who demands from you an account of the hope that is within you; yet do it with gentleness and reverence [or respect]".[55]

The words "gentleness, reverence [or respect]" should be heavily underlined. Depth of disagreement is never an excuse for aggression or discourtesy. I fear that as I look back over my life, even just applying what is said here, I will not regret the lack of opportunity for evangelism but rather the failure to take the opportunities that were there.

This whole question of involvement will necessarily raise issues of priority, and we will have to come back to that when we look in a later chapter at our relationship with our local church. For now, however, we simply have to recognise that conflicts of priority will be an issue for every Christian ambassador, especially where, as will today usually be the case, home, church and work are all in different places. My experience has been that one all too easily ends up living on the margins. I am closely involved with those with whom I work but, because of other commitments, I do not generally socialise with them. I make a specific but time-limited commitment to the church and the community in which I live, all too conscious that there will be others who think I should do more. Even the family can be squeezed, as we shall see later. The risk is that no one (including ourselves) is quite happy with the balance struck but struck it must be. Surprisingly often, God leaves us to work through our own responsibilities: there are no rules, few guidelines and even fewer Divine interventions. There is nevertheless much that has to be decided and resolved, and sometimes the Christian child really has to behave as an adult!

We have so far concentrated on the ambassador as involved

---

[55] I Peter 3 v 15–16.

in the sphere into which he or she has been called. Now we must look at the other side of the coin. Ambassadors are to be distinctive. There should be no doubt as to their culture, the government they represent or the Sovereign in whose place they stand. They will be distinctive. All that must equally apply to the Christian ambassador. Peter puts it like this:

"Beloved, I urge you as aliens and exiles to abstain from the desires of the flesh which wage war against the soul. Conduct yourselves honorably amongst the Gentiles, so that, though they may malign you as evildoers, they may see your honourable deeds and glorify God when he comes to judge."[56]

We become different, and we live differently to those amongst whom we live and work.

When I was growing up in the 1960s, a question for young Christians that we found troubling, was how we were to be distinctive in our lives. My children and grandchildren do not need to ask that question. The gulf is wide and widening. I simply want to draw attention to the context in which we live and our involvement in that context. I want also to draw attention to the difficulties that this can throw up for Christians involved in secular culture, which, as we have seen, for all its non-religious pretensions, has behind it, spiritual forces at work.

It is the fact that the first loyalty of the ambassador lies not to those to whom he is sent but to those by whom he is sent. That, of course, is true for the Christian too. It is often all too easy for our first loyalty to lie elsewhere. In one of his novels,[57] Ian McEwan has this of his central character, a High Court judge:

"And when at last, at nine thirty, one morning at the Royal Courts of Justice, she was sworn in by the Lord Chief Justice and

---

[56] I Peter 2 v 11–12.
[57] The Children Act published by Jonathan Cape 2014.

took her oath of allegiance and her Judicial Oath before two hundred of her bewigged colleagues, and as she stood proudly before them in her robes, the subject of a witty speech, she knew that the game was up, she belonged to the law as some women had once been Brides of Christ." I have known many a colleague like that, and they can be replicated in all areas of life. Yet whilst it cannot be so with ambassadors who ultimately belong elsewhere, our involvement in and commitment to the service to which we are called should externally be little different. These are difficult balances that we must all confront and strike.

Every ambassador needs withdrawal for in-service training, rest and refreshment, and many need from time to time a new posting. So it is with the Christian ambassador, and we shall explore this a little more when we look at resources. To ignore this is to risk isolation, discouragement, contamination and exhaustion, all potentially fatal to sustained faithful service. There may be some for whom one job or one challenge makes lifelong demands, but that will not be true for most who need renewed challenges and opportunities.

STEWARD

Although as a model the ambassador has had the greatest influence on me, we should consider, if briefly, the other two models — Tenant and Steward — not only because others have found them helpful but because Steward at least is readily used in conversation about the created order whether by Christians or others. After all, a vital part of God's *Shalom*, as we have noted, is vibrant right relationships between God, humanity and the whole created order.

If the earth is the Lord's, then our part in it is a gift from

God, not for us to own but of which we are to be a faithful steward. And that is to apply personally as much as it should environmentally, in that it touches our talents, time, resources and home. There are two aspects of stewardship that we should note.

First, stewardship implies accountability. It is not possible to read the New Testament without accepting that each of us will be required to give an account for the life we have lived. Our lives, the use of what we have, must always be seen in this light. Secondly, stewardship implies faithful service. Whilst distribution of gifts may be unequal, the criterion for accountability is the same: faithfulness — "Well done, good and faithful servant." That is at the heart of Jesus' principle that much will be required of those to whom much is given. Stewardship is not about playing safe. Those with five talents and two talents took risks; it was the man with one who played safe and look at what happened to him.

I was a Chancellor in the Church of England, and part of my work related to the use of churches. Most church members inherit buildings under their stewardship, and that involves passing them on to the next generation. Heritage bodies are rightly very hot on this. However, churches are not museums, but living places of worship and the layout that suited yesteryear may not be appropriate today. Risks may be inherent in stewardship as we seek to make a fine old building a place of living worship. The easy route is to play safe, but the easy route is all too rarely the Christian route of stewardship.

This stewardship model follows quite closely that of ambassador. Faithful service requires both involvement and distinctiveness. The steward is acting on behalf of the owner just as the ambassador does on behalf of the Sovereign. Each is given a wide discretion in how they do the work they have been given, and each will have to give an account of it. Both models embrace the whole of our life. They cover the use of gifts and money, the hospitality of the home and the work we do. All of these deserve individual treatment and have, of course, been written about by many others. However, in an increasingly isolated and individualistic society, I do think we need to look again at the ministry of hospitality.

There is a strong emphasis in the Bible on hospitality, whether to those who have no shelter of their own or those who need food and shelter as they exercise peripatetic Christian ministry. It all depends on the needs of the times. Once again, I need to revert to personal experience to illustrate. We had for forty-six years a large old house in central Liverpool. We have always seen this house, the only one available to us in our parish at the time, as a gift from God and, therefore, as a trust from him. There has always been room for others to stay or live there, and usually, that has been the case. We have always worked on the basis that one mark of a Christian family is that there is always room for one more. Hospitality is something that all can practise: the room at work that is a pleasure to visit; the flat where there is always time for coffee and a chat; the car owner always alert to the needs of others. The list is potentially endless.

Fostering and adoption is a species of hospitality and, whilst it is not for everyone, everyone should at least consider it. If we believe in the importance of Christian homes and families, then we should not flinch from fostering and adoption. There are lots of good materials around and well-informed organizations[58] for any Christian wanting to think through this issue. We are reminded that if every church could produce one new set of foster parents or adopters, the current childcare crisis would be solved

---

[58] For example "Home for Good" just Google!

at a stroke. Hospitality is an area where Christians have to make their own decisions because no two sets of personal circumstances are quite the same. What is important is that the claims of hospitality in all its forms are both recognised and addressed. What results from that is to be respected by others as the individual judgment of the individual Christian.

TENANT

The tenant is a less considered model. Jesus used tenant imagery rather in the way we have discussed stewardship. It is, however, to the Old Testament that we need to turn to see the model of Landlord and Tenant illustrating the relationship between God and his chosen people. [59] It is seen both in the covenant relationship between God and his people and (in what for the Jews was really one and the same thing) the enjoyment of the Promised Land. The formal covenant language of the Old Testament uses many of the concepts of the law of landlord and tenant. There is a scholarly view that the Old Testament frames the Covenant in the language of the treaties of the day between the superior power and the vassal state. This can be seen, for example, in the structure of the book of Deuteronomy. In fact, it also resembles quite closely the structure of a lease between landlord and tenant with conditions of tenancy and even a forfeiture clause. This is not the place, nor indeed am I adequately qualified, for a sustained consideration of this. However, it makes the point again that what we have is from God and is his, and he will require an account of it. It also serves as a reminder that it is all to be used as he determines. Just as a tenant holds land from his landlord on the basis of conditions, so we hold what we have

---

[59] Another strain of thought suggested by Roger Dowley.

from God on condition that its use may be determined by him and must be in accordance with his values and principally with the Golden Rule: "Do to others as you would have them do to you."[60]

Once again, these are models and not allegories; we must be cautious not to press them too hard or too far. They are also demanding, indeed sometimes troubling, models. They do no more, however, than acknowledge the true relationship between God and his adopted children. Everything that we have been considering must be seen in this light. Our choices are to be conditioned by the requirements to act justly and to love mercy. They are also to be made in the sure and certain knowledge that we must give an account and therefore to be effective, we must at all times walk humbly with our God.[61] The big picture is that the ambassador, the steward and the tenant are, as we have seen, part and parcel of the development of *Shalom* — vibrant right relationships between humans themselves, humans and the rest of the created order and, most of all, between humans and God himself.

I am conscious of repeatedly coming back to the question of giving an account. In a later chapter, I include a brief essay on a Christian lawyer's understanding of what this means. I am anxious that we do not become obsessed by it, but I think that I am even more anxious because the modern church teaches little about it even though Jesus was crystal clear that judgment would come to all.

As I have reflected on these models, I have been struck by the responsibility that God has entrusted to those who choose to

---

[60] Luke 6 v 31.
[61] Micah 6 v 8.

serve Him. Just as the master in Jesus' story of the talents did not dictate how his servants were to use what they had been given, so God expects us to take responsibility for how we serve him. God does not pull the strings of our life as though we were simply his puppets doing his bidding. He leaves us, in a very real sense, just to get on with it.

This is in no way inconsistent with the idea of God's call or his will for our lives. I believe God called me into the law and required me to specialize in those areas that most affect those at the bottom of the social pile. That said, he did not dictate to me how I was to do that; that was my side of the relationship. The ambassador works out how the job is to be done on the ground. The steward chooses how to use the resources for which he is responsible. The tenant determines the actual use of the property and the work that needs to be done. Each remains responsible for the outcome, of course.

I think we should be as wary of those who claim that their every step is specifically directed by God, just as we should be of those who have no sense of accountability to Him. Adopted children we undoubtedly are, but we are treated by God as serious adults as we seek to work out our calling and our life of obedience to Him. No wonder Paul told his friends to "work out your own salvation in fear and trembling."[62] It is not that we need to doubt our place with God, but we do have to accept responsibility for how we work out our calling in our human life.

God will sustain us in all that we do. He will encourage, equip and strengthen us for the service to which he has called us. He gave Solomon all he needed to be an outstanding ruler. He then entrusted Solomon with that charge to carry it out as he thought would be pleasing to God — or not, as his later years

---

[62] Philippians 2 v 12.

showed.

As we have surveyed the fields of the service that we have been chosen and called to undertake, I am conscious of the need for a corrective. As I have said, I have always found it relatively simple to embrace the concept of Christian servanthood, even slavery. I have always found it more difficult to practise being a child of God. It is not that I doubt his love or his care for me. It is simply how I have experienced it. Yet it remains the case that we are primarily adopted, loved and valued as children of God. Our eternal relationship with him, which he has chosen and offered to us, is not a master and servant relationship but one of loving parent and child, indeed loving friends.

These ideas are for a Christian, not, of course, mutually exclusive. The child sits at the father's table but voluntarily remains under his authority. The problem is not one of status but of feeling. The trouble with feelings is that they are variable and spasmodic. My experience is that we must simply enjoy the good ones when they come. At other times we have to hold on to promise and guaranteed status. All our thinking about the undoubted service that God asks of us must be in the context of a personal relationship where God's love and generosity far exceed anything we can imagine, let alone deserve. Paul says this:

"…And hope does not disappoint us, because God's love has been poured into our hearts through the Holy Spirit that is being given to us."[63]

That is the context of our service: our grateful acknowledgement of that free and undeserved outpouring of love. As a child loves their parents and wants to please them, so our desire to please God should be a response to our love for God together with a healthy fear or awe of God and his judgment.

---

[63] Romans 5 v 5.

CHAPTER 7

FIGHTERS: THE CONFLICTS OF CHRISTIAN LIVING

There was a televised debate at the Cambridge Union on religion. An eminent Roman Catholic layman said something in his speech that prompted antagonism in the hall. "Do I hear hissing?" He asked. "There is always hissing when the waters of heaven meet the fires of hell!" A clever riposte, but it provides a timely reminder that being salt and light will not always provoke a response, either friendly or sympathetic. To live the life of faith with integrity in a secular culture will inevitably provoke discomfort and quite often conflict.

If Christians are seriously engaged in the workplace, public institution or community, they will always be asking questions: was another treated fairly? Is this advert honest? Is this process responsible? Are these financial arrangements fair? Have we allowed profit to trump safety, fairness or quality? That is what being salt and light is all about, but not everyone will appreciate it. Sometimes our view will prevail, but sometimes, perhaps often, it will not. How does the Christian handle defeat of that sort? How do you live with integrity when you lose on something that matters to you? Can the wounded or the defeated remain on the battlefield?

Everyone's experience and response will be different, and it would be presumptuous of me to seem either to lay down what issues should be engaged or how Christians should respond to defeat on a particular question. Those are issues for each Christian to resolve as we work out our calling and as we reflect on the account that we will be required to give. We need to be able to challenge, even criticize, each other. That is one way in which we learn. We need also to encourage and support one another. Nowhere is this more so than amongst Christians engaged in the same or similar tasks. There needs to be critical solidarity amongst Christians, but there must also be proper respect for the individual judgments that each makes. The tension between staying and leaving is acute, and we will not all make the same call. We will encounter quite enough opposition in the Christian life without unnecessarily falling out with each other.

It seems to me that there are four options available to a Christian who, whilst immersed in secular culture, finds that they are in the minority on some question of significance. The first is to compartmentalize life, to withdraw that area from the influence of faith or to suspend faith in that area. That, in fact, quite often happens though it would rarely be acknowledged in such blunt terms. The second is to adopt a cynical stance: this is the way the world is, this is the way it chooses to behave; this is their problem not mine, so I must go along with it as nothing will change. I seriously question whether either approach is consistent with integrity, and I suspect that my reasons are self-evident from the ways in which I have described the options. That said, I can understand why refuge in the first is often taken. No one, however, ever promised that the Christian life would be an easy ride: quite the opposite.

The third option is withdrawal. Of course, there may come a time when no other option is compatible with integrity, but that will inevitably be at the cost of withdrawing the preservative or turning off the light. We have looked at the story of Abraham pleading for Sodom when he knew it faced judgment and the enthralling discussion between him and God about the justice of punishing all for the sins of most;[64] it ends with God saying: "For the sake of ten [righteous] I will not destroy." There were not ten such and the city was destroyed, but if there had been... The very presence of Christians can, as we have noted, be the means of blessing and protection. Withdrawal may salve the individual conscience, but it comes at a price to those around.

The fourth option is to carry on in the conviction that the overall purpose of what we are involved in (and are part of) matters more than the single issue on which we have lost. This may not be easy; others (including other Christians) may misunderstand this, but integrity may permit or even require perseverance in a dark and potentially rotting place as light and salt.

In the end Christians have to work out these issues for themselves. It seems only right, therefore, to give some brief examples of my own approach. My own experiences will, of course, be peculiar to me, but they might illustrate something of what I have been trying to express. They may even help others on their course.

My present understanding of sexual relations from Scripture is that God has given sexual intercourse to be expressed between a man and a woman united in the bond of lifelong marriage to the exclusion of all others. As those who believe and practise that do not comprise a significant number of family law litigants, the Christian who thinks as I do and who ventures into this area will inevitably experience conflict — with themselves, with other Christians and with other human beings. Such a Christian will

---

[64] Genesis 18 v 16–33.

encounter serial relationships (and sometimes polygamous ones), same-gender relationships, single-parent and same-sex families, families created by multiple relationships or IVF or surrogacy or variations of these, or indeed by means as yet unknown. There is in this area for our society an enduring tension between what we can do and what we ought to do. This is a tension generally recognised but one with which our society struggles; our technical skills far exceed our ethical skills. This is uncomfortable territory for the Christian seeking to practise family law which is really all about managing the consequences of human failure with a view to protecting the interests of those least able to protect themselves — usually the children. What then are we to do?

I could simply sever all this from my Christian life and ensure that the two do not meet, and I fear that I could find churches that would allow me to do just that, provided I was investing time and energy in their life and ministry. I could simply shrug my shoulders and say that the world is as it is, and what more could you expect? I could withdraw from this area of work altogether as other Christians have done for reasons that I respect but with which, as I have indicated, I profoundly disagree. Indeed, there are Christians who argue that the gap between divine law and secular law has now widened to the extent, particularly in family law, that the Christian conscience can no longer accommodate both and that withdrawal is the only option. I can understand why such an argument is made and have indeed sometimes felt just that way.

My continued practice as a judge of the Family Division testifies to my rejection of the arguments for withdrawal, something that I have sought more than once to justify in public.[65] In outline my reaction, both theological and intuitive, is that the People of God should be wherever humanity is hurting; child abuse and the breakdown of family relationships and all the consequences that flow from it are very painful indeed. There is, however, a further reason: these all seem to me areas of human life that cry out for the presence of salt and light, not its withdrawal. The real question is whether that can be done with integrity.

My approach is first to recognise that the principle that underpins family law is that the welfare of the child is to be the paramount consideration of the court. That seems to me a principle consistent with any Christian ethic. Next, one has to recognise that whatever views I may have about adult choice and behaviour in any particular case, there are usually children involved who had no part in the adult decisions that resulted in their existence but whose futures are profoundly affected by them. I do not think that I should desert them. My approach has been to ask whether I can leave the child in a better place than I found him or her; if so, then I will act.

The judge must look at the case from the child's perspective. I have encountered unconventional families with a real skill in caring for damaged children. The healing of the child matters more to me than the nature of the adult relationship. Moreover, in many cases, the adults concerned are the only effective parents the child has ever known, and the needs of the child require formal recognition of that relationship. The younger the child, the greater the need for that recognition; and the greater the damage that will be suffered if that need for security remains unmet. The welfare of the child is the prevailing ethic in making a choice.

---

[65] See for example my Richard O'Sullivan memorial lecture published in No 176 of Law & Justice – The Christian Law Review (Edmund Plowden Trust).

All this is, for me, well-illustrated in the difficulties we have encountered with overseas commercial surrogacy arrangements. There is no common world view on surrogacy, and each country has its own laws that range from a complete prohibition on surrogacy to an acceptance of commercial surrogacy. That whole range can be found in Europe alone. Germany, France and Italy forbid surrogacy; Russia and the Ukraine not only permit surrogacy but seem to encourage commercial surrogacy. In the UK, surrogacy is permitted but must involve no payment by way of reward, and no surrogacy agreement is legally enforceable. Accordingly, those who could afford to do so went abroad, entered into agreements that were perfectly legal there (but would not have been here) and then returned to this country and sought legal recognition of their status as parents. This is, of course, an issue faced by many countries all over the world, irrespective of political or religious tradition.

Here is not the place for a detailed legal analysis save to say that initially, all these cases were referred to me, and it became obvious that they highlighted an acute tension between public policy and the welfare of the individual child. The state was entitled to legislate in this country against commercial surrogacy and to expect the courts to uphold that policy. However, there was now a real child with real needs who had no part in the choices that the parents had made. In my view, welfare will almost always trump policy, but it was a distinctively uncomfortable exercise. Perhaps that discomfort is best illustrated by some words I used in the leading early case on this subject:

"I feel bound to observe that I find this process of authorization most uncomfortable. What a court is required to do is to balance two competing and potentially irreconcilably conflicting concepts. Parliament is clearly entitled to legislate against commercial surrogacy and is clearly entitled to expect that the court should implement that policy consideration in its decisions. Yet it is also recognised that as the full rigour of that policy consideration will bear on one wholly unequipped to comprehend it let alone to deal with its consequences (i.e., the child concerned) that rigor must be mitigated by the application of a consideration of that child's welfare. That approach is both humane and intellectually coherent. The difficulty is that it is almost impossible to imagine a set of circumstances in which by the time the case comes to court, the welfare of any child (particularly a foreign child) would not be gravely compromised (at the very least) by a refusal to make an order."[66]

In considering these matters, I have thought often of the Irish stationmaster who, when asked how to get to Tralee, said that he would not start from here! A judge has to start from where the parties are; discomfort is unavoidable.

This has been a personal journey. I have had to justify to myself that being a Judge of the Family Division remains a possible Christian vocation. For the reasons set out above I have done that, though whether others are convinced remains a moot point.

Other Christians who travel a similar route may find it easier either because they understand Scripture differently or they find it easier to integrate the issues that have troubled me. I think that what I have come to understand from my own experience is that we can live with Christian integrity on a field on which we may have felt defeated or seriously compromised, and we can do so by concentrating on a greater good, the loss of which would be

---

[66] Re X & Y (FOREIGN SURROGACY) [2008] EWHC 3030 (Fam) at para 24.

much worse than the discomfort of our conscience. The overall good purpose in which we are involved does not become the less good because there are difficulties and blemishes along the way.

There are two other factors to be fed into this discussion. The first is a proper respect for the rights of others to make choices about their lifestyle. In God's world, human beings take personal responsibility for their life choices and will be accountable for that. I am not uncomfortable with a law that enables people to do that, at least within the limits required by the needs for social co-existence. That entails a respect for the choices of others even where agreement or approval must be withheld. The truth is that good must be chosen; it cannot be imposed. That does not mean to say that I must have a blank mind and a silent voice. I have rarely been guilty of either. It does mean understanding where responsibility for decisions lies and acknowledging that. I have found some support from Paul's comment to his friends in Corinth:

"I wrote to you in my letter not to associate with sexually immoral persons — not at all meaning the immoral of this world or the greedy and robbers, or idolaters, since you would then need to go out of the world."[67]

He clearly did not intend that they should. He understood the tension between involvement and distinctiveness.

Secondly, Christians need a proper sense of their own fallibility and few need that more than does the judge. It is not for us to look condescendingly down on the failures of others (or worse still, like the Pharisee, disparagingly) but to remember that we too fail. When tempted to such an attitude, I like to remember Jesus' words about adultery and lust.[68] It is hard to leave those with a self-satisfied air. I have been struck by the essential

---

[67] I Corinthians 5 v 9–10.
[68] Matthew 5 v 27–28.

equality of humanity in the eyes of God: I am of no greater value to God nor loved any more by Him than the worst offender in the dock of my court, and I need the Cross every bit as much as does that offender.

Furthermore, these are rarely battles conducted in private. Others may have much to say about the position we decide to take. Secularists may complain that a Christian holding secular office should not be entertaining these issues at all. They are right in the sense that I should not impose my values on those who appear in my court. They are wrong insofar as they suggest that judges should personally embrace secular values in their field of work or, worse still, have no values at all. The value-free judge could not, does not and should not exist.

Likewise, Christians complain that I do not stand up clearly for what is right and indeed that I am complicit in what they see as plainly wrong. They are right to draw attention to this. It is a matter worth debating, and, after all, I may be wrong sometimes. They are wrong insofar as they suggest that every Christian in authority has the right or duty to impose on others standards that those others have chosen not to follow or that the Christian should simply withdraw. As we have seen, just as the church comprises volunteers, so we must respect the fact that we serve a God who has given to human beings the right and responsibility to make their own choices. The judge in a secular system is simply acknowledging that. That is not to say that anything goes or that a judge must always be silent. It merely, in practice at least, acknowledges that for me, the welfare of the child will usually trump my disapproval of or unease at any adult conduct.

The judge's own views will, however, inevitably feed into a discretionary decision about what promotes the welfare of the child. Yet whilst the judge's own values will be relevant, they have to be considered alongside the values of society (insofar as they can be discerned) and the values of the family concerned. I grew up in the middle years of the last century in a world almost unrecognisable through contemporary eyes. This becomes very clear when trying to describe it to students or young lawyers. It was then still possible to talk about the agreed norms or common values of society. Not everyone, of course, lived by them, but there was a consensus in favour of marriage, against divorce and of children being born in wedlock. Today it is difficult to discern any such consensus.

The values of the judge will be relevant but may not be decisive. As an example, let us take a dispute between parents, one of whom is a Muslim, and one is not, over whether their son should be circumcised. I may have views about male circumcision, but there is no overall view in our society, and accordingly, the views of that part of the family in which the child is mainly to live may have to be treated as decisive. On the other hand, where female genital mutilation is in issue, the views of society (and on this there is a broad consensus) and the judge will prevail over those of the family. Again, if one considers the physical punishment of children, that divides all sectors of society, whether by age, gender, race or class, and the judge, whatever views he may hold, may be unable to insist on more than compliance with the criminal law and otherwise leave the matter to parental decision or if necessary to that of the individual parent, if they cannot agree.

I acknowledge that this was a long discussion of personal experience, but I know of no better way of illustrating the conflicts that may arise from being salt and light. I could have described others, but it would only have been at second-hand. I have hinted at some of these for those in business, education, health, retail, care and others. Everyone will have their own experience and their own stories. My purpose is simply to try to shed some light on understanding what can happen as we faithfully seek to be salt and light where God has placed us. My hope is that any light so shed may help illuminate the thinking of others in respect of their own lives.

As we wrestle with living the faith with integrity in our society, there is one further area of conflict arising out of all this to which we should now return. In many of its aspects it will be familiar to all Christians. It is an area that we have met before and will encounter again, and it is one in which I have very much less confidence in my own approach: the conflict of priorities in the Christian life. I may be called to be spouse and parent, Reader and church leader, to provide professional services voluntarily and to be a career lawyer. However, the number of hours in the day does not expand to accommodate extra commitments, even if we can get better at using the time available. I do not think that I have ever really achieved a satisfactory balance and so have lived a bit nearer the edge of each area of my life than I would have liked. Indeed, I have wondered whether any such balance is achievable at all that would have allowed me to contribute to each area as well as I would have wanted. Theoretically, I dare say that it must be possible; I simply have not found it. Judging from most of those I have known, that represents a majority experience amongst Christians. I think that we must be alert to this — others involved in our lives will certainly be so. Maybe we just have to accept that attempted perfection is the enemy of the good. In the end, each of us must do the best we can wherever we are.

No Christian was ever promised an easy life: on offer is simply the way of the Cross. However, we were promised a life of opportunity to serve God, life in all its fullness, and we were promised the resources to do that. It is to these that we must now turn.

CHAPTER 8

RESOURCES FOR CHRISTIAN LIVING

What I have tried to sketch out as the normal Christian life of the ordinary layperson is, in reality, deeply demanding. It covers every aspect of life both in terms of what we do and what we say and think. It is something (like marriage) "not to be enterprised nor taken in hand unadvisedly, lightly or wantonly but reverently, discreetly, soberly and in the fear of God."[69] Where then will we find the resources necessary to equip and sustain us in our calling?

God promises that where he calls so he will equip. This was true of Moses as it was of Elijah when he was rescued from what appears to have been a severe bout of depression.[70] It remains true of the God of the New Testament who desires that his people be equipped for every good work to which they are called. I have found myself coming back time and again to these words in the letter to the Hebrews:

"For we do not have a high priest who is unable to sympathize with our weakness, but we have one who in every respect has been tested as we are, but without sin. Let us, therefore, approach the throne of grace with boldness, so that we may receive mercy and find grace to help in time of need."[71]

---

[69] Book of Common Prayer 1662.
[70] I Kings 19.
[71] Hebrews 4 v 15–16.

The ambassador, though trusted with much, is never abandoned to his or her own devices.

But where are these resources to be found? I think we need to start with a negative. However important it is that every Christian should be and remain a member of the worshipping community, we usually will not find all that we need in our local church. Why should we? Those who lead may well have no experience of what occupies our daily life and little insight into the questions that trouble us. This is no criticism, it is merely an acceptance of reality. It follows that most (indeed, I think I would say all) of us must take responsibility for seeing that we are adequately resourced. What follows is intended to help in the fulfilment of that responsibility.

I am not, of course, saying that the local church has no role at all. There we can learn and practise the essence of our faith. There we can learn to fulfil our general vocation to become the person God created us to be. It is when we address the details of our specific vocation that we will experience the limitations of the local church. It is here that we will have to take specific responsibility for our own resourcing.

It will be different for each one of us. As a lawyer and judge operating in a deeply secular culture with a system that has moved far from conventional Christian ethics, I have particular needs that will not apply to others. In a real sense that will be true for each of us: we will all have our own particular needs. The needs of the retail worker, financier, government official, school governor, farmer and businessperson will be different, and one may not always understand the other.

What follows is inevitably highly influenced by my own experience, but much of it cuts across in practice a wide field of experience and will, therefore (so I hope) make it helpful for others too. It does, however, assume that all of us as good ambassadors have come thoroughly to understand the culture in which we work and how that differs from the culture of the Kingdom of God from where we have been sent. I very much doubt that lawyers are alone in finding that gap is not only widening but also doing so at an accelerating pace.

So we turn to the resources available to us. I cannot, of course, be too detailed; oceans of ink and vast amounts of learning have been expended on Bible study and prayer. I aim to do no more than hopefully offer some helpful hints.

My principal resource is the Bible. I think we must start with Paul's assertion to Timothy:

"All Scripture is inspired by God and is useful for teaching, for reproof, for correction and for training in righteousness, so that everyone who belongs to God may be proficient, equipped for every good work."[72]

I know that this passage creates endless arguments about the authority of Scripture. This is not the place to debate this issue. I hold a fairly traditional, conservative position that requires me to treat Scripture as God's authoritative word. The passage is, however, crucially important in describing the purpose of Scripture — the equipping of Christians for service.

Whatever specific theological position we take on the authority of Scripture, and assuming that we are at least going to take it seriously, we have to recognise that many of the issues with which we have to deal would have been unknown to the original writers and their readers or hearers. We cannot, therefore, just read across literally from then till now without taking account of that. Thus, an acceptance of the authority of Scripture does not relieve me of the need to interpret it into

---

[72] II Timothy 3 v 16–17.

today's setting so that I may be proficient and equipped for the specific service to which I have been called. That must be as true for all others as it is for me.

How then do we go about this? It seems to me that it is a threefold process. First, what did this mean, or how did it sound to its original hearers? (This is known as exegesis.) Then secondly, what principles of life and thought can be drawn from it as originally understood? (This is known as exposition.) And finally, how can those principles be made to work in the world in which I find myself? (This is application). Often, I will need help to do this. I do not have the original languages and only a limited understanding of the cultures in which they were used. I shall, therefore, almost always need help in exegesis, whether from commentaries, the preaching and teaching of the local church or from those who have made a study of these issues. That may often be true of exposition as well, though as we work at this, so we will acquire our own skills in discerning the principles to be derived from exegesis. It is the third stage where we are most likely to be left on our own and where mistakes may be more likely. As we will see, we may find help from those who walk or have walked in our specific calling. It is, however, at this point that we may have to accept the responsibility of exercising personal judgment. The risk of error is inherent in the normal Christian life. It is a risk that does not excuse inaction, but it does repeatedly remind us that mercifully we are justified by faith and not by our works.

I remember Roger Dowley (mentioned earlier) once leading a Bible study on the Good Shepherd in John 10. Now it was a story with which I was familiar and had been taught it as assurance that I belonged eternally to God. I had not particularly noticed, let alone questioned, the hostile reaction of the Jewish leaders in verses 19 to 21 and later in verse 31. I had always absorbed the story as a mark of God's love for his people. This study, however, focused on the bad shepherds of Ezekiel 34, and the contrast between the bad shepherding of the leadership and the good shepherding of God and the judgment inherent in this. Once seen, of course, it fully explains the reaction to Jesus, for what was being heard was that the judgment of Ezekiel 34 was about to be fulfilled. It was a very long way from the warm and comforting thoughts that that teaching of Jesus had hitherto induced in me. What is more, the study very strongly suggested that whilst my present thoughts were fine as far as they went, there was rather more to this teaching than I had up till then understood. Exegesis had transformed exposition, and that in turn raised issues of application that had not occurred to me. Justice stands very close to the heart of God. I had instinctively grasped that this was so but had not really understood how close it truly was.

Another insight, in part derived from Roger but found in many other places too, relates to seeing the story of the Bible as an overarching narrative. We have already noted the outlines of that story. All Scripture forms a part of the overarching story and needs to be read and understood as such. In truth, Genesis 1–4 provides an almost complete philosophical and theological account of the world as we find it to be. There is the created order turned to disorder by human choice. There are subtle mixtures of good and evil in the Garden and the apparent triumph of evil again through human choice. Human choice also allows the apparent triumph of hate over love as Cain kills his brother in a fit of jealousy. Overall, we can see both the allure of sin and the love and justice of the Creator. Humanity has chosen its path, and it is not God's. For the resolution of those issues, we have to look at the rest of the book.

We do, however, need to recognise this: if we are to be instructed by Scripture, we do need to read it. With an increasing church tradition of one service a week, we will have a very distorted view of Scripture if we rely only on hearing it then. We need to make time to read it. There are many guides to reading the Bible, and each person must make their own decision as to what is best for them. My only comment would be that sometimes we should read long passages or even whole books so that we retain the concept of an overarching narrative.

And we need to read it with two key Christian concepts clearly in mind. First, the Holy Spirit is given to us as a guide, as Jesus promised on the night before he died: "When the Spirit of truth comes, he will guide you into all truth."[73] We need to notice here his role in understanding the Scriptures. The second is that both the Scriptures and Jesus are described as the Word of God. Now the theological ramifications of this are far outside my field of competence, but they do remind me that the Word of God is a living instrument and not just an historic text. It is capable, therefore, of speaking into situations that could never have been in the mind of the original writer. That is the role, under the Spirit, of exposition and application.

That reminder that the Word is living prompts one further thought. Although I seek to argue for an ordered approach to understanding the Bible through this threefold process, I fully recognise that the Spirit is not constrained by this. All Christians probably have had the experience of being hit by a verse that speaks directly to some current issue in their life but with a sense that would surprise both scholar and original writer. As one who has been blessed by such an experience, I do not in any way want

---

[73] John 16 v 13.

to undermine that though I do want to say that, whilst it may be a good supplement, it is no substitute for ordered study and reflection.

Prayer is the lifeblood of the Christian pilgrimage. However, not many of us find it easy; indeed, I doubt that I am alone in all too often experiencing a sense of failure in it. I was brought up in a strong tradition of the daily "quiet time", in which I have sadly proved myself an endemic failure. Every so often, I persist, but most of the time, I fail. And that sense of failure is compounded by the richness of the prayer life that others seem to enjoy from this discipline. That is, of course, not a criticism of that tradition, though it may be a warning against a one-size-fits-all approach to prayer. The Ignatian assertion — "Pray as you can and not as you can't (or not as you think you ought)" was liberating not because it excused failure but because it offered hope for the future.

It is not that I stopped praying. I have always found strength in corporate prayer, whether liturgical or in a prayer meeting. It was private prayer I found so hard. Though even there I found relief. I learnt many years ago to practise the Presence of Christ so that wherever I was and whatever I was doing, I was conscious of being in the presence of Christ. That was as true of the courtroom as of the church, of my study as of my living room and of the judges' dining room as of the prayer meeting. I was open to and aware of the Spirit's suffusing my life — body, mind and spirit. I was also acutely aware that I was accountable to Him for whatever it was that I was then doing. In this area I, like I suppose all others, remain a learner.

I have been asked whether I used to pray about the cases in which I was involved. The answer is mixed. I always pray about the office of judge to which I believe I was called, and always I pray for wisdom, fairness and the ability to treat all as befits those made in the image of God. I acknowledge my equality before God with any who appear in my court. I do not, however, pray to see the correct outcome in a specific case. There are, I think, two reasons for this: first, because I believe that God has equipped me and given me the responsibility to decide the case; and secondly, because God should not be lumbered with responsibility for my mistakes — that belongs to me and to me alone. Those two reasons may well apply to everyone engaged in decision-making in a secular culture. Our Christian calling, for all our status as the adopted children of God, is a seriously adult undertaking.

I am clearly not the person to write about proficiency in prayer. Fortunately, there are many who are. My purpose, from the perspective of the layperson engaged in secular culture, is simply to underline the importance of prayer in the sustaining of our specific vocation. On the basis of the Ignatian insight, each of us is responsible for deciding how we do it; my concern is simply that we do it. I have found it a great help over the years to have a spiritual director. That is not someone to tell me what to think or pray but someone sensitive to my spiritual needs and skilled in discerning a response to them. Experience has indeed taught me that prayer is the lifeblood of the Christian pilgrimage.

The next key resource is our fellow Christians. They really come into three categories. Those who support us personally; those who work in the same field as we do; and those whose learning and insight can light up our way ahead. Each should be considered in turn in the context of a strong New Testament, and indeed biblical, emphasis on the mutual interdependence of the people of God. In Galatians 6, Paul points up the critical balance between personal responsibility — don't compare yourself with others (v 4–5) — and mutual interdependence — carrying one another's burden (v2). That chapter (especially v 1–10) will always repay study on this point as each of us seeks the right balance in our own life.

In one sense, those who support us are the most important group, being the ones who love us, encourage us, pray for us and generally keep us on the straight and narrow. Many of us will be fortunate enough that that includes our own family. Their failure to share the world's reverence of us can open the door to uncomfortable but necessary truth. It very much includes members of our local church, and I know (though they do not) how much I owe them for their prayerful support over the years, even when they have had little more than an inkling of what it is I have been doing. Although it can be stated shortly, we should never underestimate this God-given resourcing of our service. That said, we should never expect more from it than it can actually give. Many of us (though happily not all) find that how we spend our week rarely, if at all, features in Sunday prayers and yet many not so featured often need prayer support more than those who regularly appear. It is a salutary reminder that so often we must find our own resources.

The importance of Christians with whom we work either in employment or in the voluntary sector, or in the community is that they understand, in a way which our local church and its leadership may not, the real issues that confront us. My experience of Christians in the law is that they are essentially supportive of each other though, as we have seen, not always in agreement. I have hugely valued the Christian lawyers whom I have known, whether or not we disagree over specific questions, because there is a general acknowledgment that we are all trying, however fallibly, to be faithful witnesses and ambassadors in this world. Sometimes real difficulty and conflict can arise, but I have valued their prayer, their support, their challenges to my views and their encouragement. I hope too that I have been of some positive value to them.

Those experiences embolden me to say that all Christians working in a secular culture should make time for one another. It does not need to be the formal structure that lawyers, doctors and others have adopted; it simply requires Christians to make time for one another. An important moment in the week for me was when a small number gathered every Wednesday lunchtime in our court building in Liverpool to pray for our work and profession. It was a nice touch that we often had to meet in the Witness Waiting Room. I have discovered that all this is, however, easier said than done. To make time for one another does not always sit easily with the time required by our local church and others, and Christians do not find that apparent conflict of loyalties easy to address. It is not difficult to see why, when that conflict is not always viewed sympathetically by church leaders and others who also want our time and energy. I think that all I can say is that time given to those Christians in our area of activity is time well spent in terms of resourcing our service as ambassadors.

Then there are the Christians with expertise who light up the way ahead. They come in all sorts. Some are fairly obvious: local leaders and teachers, those who write commentaries on the Bible or who produce what are really handbooks for Christian living. Some are less obvious as we look among those who perhaps work in the same area and culture as we do. I have discovered that lawyers, for example, often read the Bible with spectacles different from those of professional theologians. My understanding of being a Christian lawyer in a secular culture has been greatly enriched by books like Roger Dowley's "The Lost Bequest", David McIlroy's "A Biblical View of Law and Justice", and Jonathan Burnside's "God, Justice and Society". I would hope others could find such writers in their field.

Some came (to me at least) as a surprise. Some years ago, after much experience of failing to give up something in Lent, I took instead to reading a big theological book. This all too often turned out not to be the easy option. They have all been illuminating, but Tom Wright's magnum opus on Paul, Christopher Wright's "Old Testament Ethics", and Kenneth Bailey's "Jesus through Middle Eastern Eyes" and "Paul through Mediterranean Eyes" would be among the highlights. They have not, for the most part, answered my pressing direct questions, but they have profoundly informed the background within which I think and act and understand and practise my faith.

What this whole process can do is to form a Christian mind and a Christian instinct, both of which are of crucial importance in decision-making in a secular culture. I was first exposed to this as a student when I read Harry Blamires' "The Christian Mind". It is crucial that every part of our mind is open to the instruction and insight of the Holy Spirit. He illustrated in a later book, "The Secularist Heresy", how we can also become numbed by the secularist assumptions of our society to which the Christian mind needs to be alert and to be equipped to challenge. Some years ago, at a conference, I remember a Cambridge Professor of Theology using the expression of a Christian having "a mind stamped with the imprint of Christ". That very neatly summarized the essence of both the Christian mind and Christian instinct. All this background material does not usually provide individual answers to specific questions, but it does cultivate a mind that thinks Christianly, and it does hone a Christian instinct.

Thus equipped, we can be more confident as we address the specific issues that confront us day by day.

I believe that a Christian instinct is a seriously undervalued resource. Most important decisions may be framed by logic, but they are not decided by it. Those decisions are much more often judgments based on evidence, as indeed most scientific theories are, initially at least. Some decisions inevitably have an instinctual component. Where to live, whom to marry, whether to change a job, whether to refuse medical treatment are all decisions with an instinctive element. We simply do not decide our personal relationships as Pythagoras proved the relationship between sides and angles of a triangle. Something more than a clear, logical mind is involved. It is this something more, which I have called instinct, that should also be open to the Spirit. My own reflection is that Christians should be more willing to trust their instinct than is often the case. Nowhere is this more so than when important decisions have to be taken under pressure of time. I have confronted this at work when faced with decisions concerning urgent medical treatment, and, of course, such decisions may, in a family context, confront any of us. There are legions of lesser decisions that each of us will meet from time to time as we seek to be faithful ambassadors. Instinct honed by experience, study and, above all, by the Holy Spirit is, to me, a key Christian asset and resource.

Every ambassador needs both to be kept up-to-date on the job and also occasionally to be withdrawn for rest and refreshment. Prayer, studying the scripture and the support of fellow Christians are all essential resources for learning and surviving on the job. We will, however, need occasionally to be withdrawn. Holidays are often a good time for a conference, a retreat or a book, but they are also a time for refreshing personal relationships. Colleagues used to complain (and I sympathize) that the first week of a holiday was taken up with domestic issues that had been deferred in the busyness of working life. I have often complained about how rarely I sat down with friends without at least an informal agenda. Our supporters do need our time. Times of withdrawal are a necessary part of the normal Christian life not only to give our supporters time but, more importantly, to make some leisured time with God. A retreat can be an excellent way to do this.

We have thought about fellow Christians as a God-given resource in our pilgrimage. And so they are. However, we should never lose the capacity to learn from others as well. I have learnt much over the years about concern for others from those who would never describe themselves as Christians. That includes friends and colleagues, but it is true in a wider context. No doubt we should be more cautious in accepting everything they say, but people of goodwill who share our aims within a secular culture may be allies, supporters and teachers too. God is not restricted. As the Masai Christians used to say — "Our God is a lion". We do not control where he is or what he does. If His People are not at work where His heart is, then He can still work, as he did through "Cyrus my Shepherd"[74] in the restoration of Israel after the exile. Christians do not take God into secular culture, they find him there already at work, work we should be careful to understand. We join God at his gracious invitation as partners in the work already underway. There is no God-forsaken part of his world.

As we reflect on the resources that are available to us, there is one word of caution to keep in mind. Much that we have to deal with today would have been unknown to the biblical writers,

---

[74] Isaiah 44 v 28.

109

and thus we are drawn into interpretation and judgment as we seek God's way in our culture. Although we have the Holy Spirit as our guide, our inherent fallibility means that we will not always get it right. Oliver Cromwell addressed the General Assembly of the Church of Scotland thus: "I beseech you, in the bowels of Christ, think it possible you may be mistaken." That is a question (and an attitude) we should keep in mind. It is the reason why humility is an essential Christian characteristic. St Paul, in addressing controversies in the church, said: "Let all be fully convinced in their own minds."[75] Error, however, remains a possibility. I have to accept that some things of which I am presently convinced may turn out to be wrong. It is a consequence of being human. We should not forget that.

---

[75] Romans 14 v 5.

CHAPTER 9

THE LAYPERSON IN THE CHURCH

The "Laos" of God are, of course, the whole people of God, whether ordained or not. However, in today's church, we have adopted the modern idiom of using lay to contrast with expert; within the community of the church, we have now come to use *lay* to distinguish between those who are ordained and those who are not. In this chapter, I am using *layperson* to describe one who is not ordained. That, however, is really all it does: it tells us nothing about the contribution that person makes.

When I was Chair of Readers in the Liverpool diocese, now over thirty years ago, we undertook a survey of readers and their individual ministries. One of the results of a well-supported survey was that readers were divided almost equally in terms of their time contribution to the church in which they were licensed. One half were to all intents, honorary curates, whereas the other half had a distinct, but time-limited, contribution to make as teachers and preachers. I understand that the picture in the diocese today remains very similar. Indeed, this split would, I think, reflect a very much larger part of the laity than just readers. All churches have those who make an endless, unstinting time commitment and those who make a real commitment but on a strictly time-limited basis. The church, of course, needs both. It is, however, the second group that I mainly have in mind. This essentially comprises those who have a serious Christian commitment but whose obligations, whether work, community involvement or care of others, necessarily limit the time they have available to their local church.

Many of us in this group can feel uneasy (if not actually guilty) about it, when we see all that others are doing. I very much hope that all that we have been reflecting on in this book will demonstrate that such unease and guilt are wholly misplaced. That, however, does not make it unreal. We need to recognise that as we consider our proper place within the people of God.

Our Christian ministry is not to be judged by time spent in the service of the church but by our faithfulness to the specific calling God has given us. That calling may well involve much time plunged in secular rather than church culture. The Foreign Office does not withdraw ambassadors to run Whitehall; it runs Whitehall so as to service ambassadors overseas. And so should the church. That said, we have seen how being salt of the earth is in part to be a full member of the worshipping community. And to be a full member of such a community means contributing to it with time, talent and money. I have always enjoyed a comment made by a former Chief Rabbi when asked about his politics: "in traditions, Conservative; in good works, Labour; in giving, Liberal." My purpose is to explore these contributions whilst recognising that many others have written extensively on them.

Paul said: "For by the grace given to me I say to everyone among you not to think of yourselves more highly than you ought to think, but to think with sober judgment, each according to the measure of faith that God has assigned." [76] Now we are all familiar with those who think too much of themselves, but I believe we have a real issue in the modern Western church of Christians who seriously undervalue the contribution that they

---

[76] Romans 12 v 3.

have to make. Sometimes that may be because they want to avoid commitment, but its usual cause is more closely aligned to a loss of confidence. It is the second part of Paul's comment that we should take to heart: to be realistic not only as to the gifts and experiences that God has given us but the contribution that those could make to the life of the church. It is that on which I would like to build.

It follows that first we will have to establish our priorities. Once we have established the contribution we might make, then we shall have to exclude the things that we cannot therefore do. Until very recently, I have eschewed almost entirely church politics — synods and everything connected with them. I have done so not because I disapprove of church politics (we really do need people who can do that well), but because my priority has been teaching and preaching, and I could not do both well at the same time. Those priorities will not only be very different for different people, but they may vary at different stages of life. What is likely always to be necessary is some choice of priorities. Of course, we will consult others in making those choices, but in the end, the choice (and the responsibility for it) will be ours alone.

Now, of course, we must remember that in making such choices, we cannot overlook some basic obligations. We need to make time to be part of the worshipping community, and we do need to make time to be part of the mutual caring and concern that should be a feature of such a community. We cannot escape these obligations by pleading some higher calling. To do so would be rather like Pharisees pledging their wealth to the Temple when they should have been using it to care for their elderly parents, an act roundly condemned by Jesus.[77]

---

[77] Mark 7 v 9–13.

Our obligation to worship and to nurture our own spiritual life should never be underestimated. We have seen how being salt of the earth must also have us as part of the worshipping community. We need to be sustained by sacrament, liturgy, prayer and music and taught by the Word. These are ways in which we can be nourished by the Holy Spirit and encouraged by others as we work out our own Monday to Saturday vocation. In this respect, I am no advocate of any particular denomination or worship-style. Each must find what works best for them. What matters is that an effective "sent" or "dispersed" church needs to be firmly grounded in the "gathered" church. In practice, you cannot have one without the other.

It follows that our key task is to discern what particular contribution each of us can make to the life of the worshipping community. In some cases, it may actually be a work skill like facility with money or organisation or learning. That, of course, needs to be balanced by our need for refreshment too. A church that assumes that a busy teacher is keen to run the Sunday school may be making a wholly unreasonable demand. In other cases, it will be a skill otherwise acquired: skill with children or young people, skill in leading a group, a great reading or singing voice or other musical talent, or just a born administrator. What matters is that we discern this skill and give it sufficient priority that it can be deployed to best advantage. It is all too easy in a discussion like this once again to create the impression that what is most needed is professional skill. I do not believe that for one moment. Of course, professional skills have their place and uses, but service in the church needs human love, compassion and time above all else, and that is not conditioned by educational background. There is an important role in the ministry of every local church for every committed believer.

Some of these contributions can be more subtle. A lawyer, for example, may be good at discerning the real issue underlying the discussion or at seeing a common thread running through it. Others will have great sensitivity or emotional intelligence that is essential to the smooth working of the Fellowship. Some contributions may be more specific in focus. Someone may have a real interest in climate change or debt relief or perhaps in some overseas project that may enrich the life and ministry of the church. Erica and I were for many years much involved in a small orphanage/school project in Malawi, and the church has been enriched both by involvement with that and contact with the Malawian pastor who ran the project.

Sometimes a layperson may be able to do something that it would be difficult for clergy to start. When we arrived in Everton in 1974, there was still a strong Orange/Green divide between the Protestant and Catholic communities. Although the City Council had taken steps to break up housing ghettos, feelings remained strong. In the course of our involvement in community affairs, two matters became plain: first, that almost all those involved in community leadership were in church on Sunday (but not the same one); and secondly, part of addressing this divide was that active Christians on both sides should be seen to do things together. As described in Chapter 4 above, we were able to start a Bible study group in our house for both sides, which the clergy supported but did not lead (indeed initially rightly decided not to attend). As it became established, they did attend but did not lead. That initiative set in train events, which with warm support from successive clergy and bishops, has transformed those relationships in our area.

The truth is that individual contributions come in many more than fifty-seven varieties. They can enrich and be appreciated by the church. The preacher, immersed for much of life in secular culture, may bring a quite different perspective to that of the ordained church leader. They may read Scripture through different spectacles, and I want to offer some examples of that in the next chapter.

Yet in the midst of all this, it is crucial for the Christian layperson to remind themselves that they have a job, they have a family, and they need some space. I am only too aware that the more we offer to our local church, the more it tends to ask of us. We should be careful about complaining, for those who ask may not appreciate all the demands on us, but we do need to be realistic. One of the areas of church life that has recently expanded is the number worshipping in our cathedrals. There are many positive reasons why that may be so, but amongst those reasons is the anonymity that a cathedral affords: there is no real risk of being asked to do more than you want. The experience of the local church can be quite different.

Now, this is important if it is to be part of our ministry and witness to do our job as well as we can, and to have a proper family life, a place where children can flourish and thus a place where parenting time is crucial. I fear that sometimes local churches, in their enthusiasm and need to be an effective body, are not properly recognising this, are guilty of something for which Jesus took the Pharisees to task: "They tie up heavy burdens, hard to bear, and lay them on the shoulders of others; but they themselves are unwilling to lift a finger to move them."[78] It is not done deliberately, but it can feel very oppressive nevertheless.

We, of course, retain responsibility for our work and family. We may need to protect them against over-strident demands. At

---

[78] Matthew 23 v 4.

the same time, we can take action ourselves. Although when our children were small, we retained many church and community commitments, we were able to ensure that we ate in the early evening as a family and were able to have unhurried bedtimes. For a while, we lived as a group of two families with up to seven young children. Although I would not have missed it for anything, no one should rush into such an arrangement, but it did leave three adults available each evening. Because our children went to school locally, they could be walked to primary school and use the bus for secondary school. That meant not having to be up too early, and so Erica and I could give each other regular time late in the evening. Happily, I did not have to leave home to serve as a High Court judge till our youngest was eighteen. It is possible to build in protected time for families, but the tension of priorities will always be present in a more or less acute form.

One of my judicial mentors in Liverpool was a senior Jewish judge deeply involved in his local community but also an outstanding family law judge. I remember asking him one day how he would react if he were offered an appointment on the High Court Bench (that could not happen now, but it was the way then). He thought for a while and then said that he knew he would not be able to refuse but, he added, "That is why every day in Shul, I pray that no one will ask." Happily for him (though less so for family law), his prayer was answered. I know how he felt.

There is one other aspect of being a layperson whose time is much spent in secular culture, which is not altogether comfortable but which we should confront. Not everyone sees things from our perspective; not everyone may agree with our priorities or be prepared to accept our choices. We may find not only that we have critics but that these critics are amongst Christians whom we value. We had to deal with some who thought that, because of where we lived and how we ordered our lives, we were sacrificing our children to our principles, and, in fairness, I could see why they might think that. I suspect that all of us will, in one way or another, be forced to defend our priorities and choices. Just as pressure to be ordained made me think through carefully my vocation as a lawyer, so one of the advantages of such pressures was to make one think through again the basis on which priorities and choices are decided. I found myself drawn, to my surprise, to that strange story of Abraham's almost-sacrifice of his son.[79] This is one of those Old Testament stories that tend to lose their impact because we know the outcome. Picture Abraham on his way to the mountain with Isaac and being stopped and questioned by a social worker from the land of Moriah. I doubt Isaac would have been allowed to go another step. It was a truly shocking enterprise. Yet the effect of the story was to make me realise that God loved my children more than I ever could and that, in being obedient to his calling, I must trust that he would look after them. I believe that that trust has been amply repaid, though of course, they must have the final word on that.

Now that was my route; you will find your own. What is certain is that at some point or other, we shall have to define and defend our priorities and choices. Once again, we have to recognise that no one ever promised that the Christian life would be easy but only that it would yield life in all its fullness.

I do not think that I should leave this subject without some thoughts about those who, although having demanding secular jobs, assume significant leadership positions in the church, whether as a self-supporting ordained minister or Catholic deacon or as a pastor in churches where formal ordination is not

---

[79] Genesis 22 v 1–19.

required. Although this forms no part of my own experience (other than having had to consider it), I know well some of those who have found themselves in that position. Much has been written about this (most of it anecdotal), and I am not competent to offer more than some thoughts provoked by my own experience and my own knowledge of the experience of others.

We must start by emphasising again both that every individual Christian is responsible for discerning (usually in association with others) and acting on God's call to them and also that the rest of the congregation should respect that discernment and the decisions that flow from it. Our views, if sought, may be offered, but that is as far as it should go. God alone knows the true purpose of his Call.

Clearly, those who respond to such a call as this must invest significant time and energy in fulfilling it. It may have implications for the time that they can give to their work, but that will have been a critical part of the discernment process. When I explored this option as a young man, my then Rector's firm advice was to discern whether God actually wanted me as the lawyer or as an ordained clergyman. He clearly saw the risk of my trying to ride two fast-paced horses. For me that advice was sound, but God may (and does) speak differently to others.

I recognise that there are those who combine secular work with formal church leadership and do so in accordance with a properly discerned call from God. In doing so, they take on particular difficulties. Of course they have hard choices over priorities. They also run the risk of criticism both from work and church leadership colleagues either that they are not pulling their weight or that they cannot really be trusted with proper responsibility. These can be painful and deeply frustrating tensions.

They can only be resolved by that person making clear the priorities that have been chosen and then by other Christians both trusting that choice and allowing that person all the scope in a ministry that those choices will actually allow. To demand too much leads to dissatisfaction with the quality of work actually done, or even burnout. To ask too little may breed frustration and discouragement. Both will impair God's plan for that person.

I acknowledge that there is a real role both in the church and in the secular culture of work for such a ministry. It does produce very difficult balances, and many find themselves frustrated, especially by the response of fellow Christians. It is, of course, entirely proper to confront Christians with a challenge to consider such a calling. In its turn, however, that imposes a responsibility not only to accept the discernment of that calling but also not even to make it unless there has been a clear thinking through of how that ministry could be developed without either making impossible demands or producing frustration.

This is a very difficult area and one that is still being explored. The anecdotal writings that I have come across suggest that we still have much to learn as to how to make the best of this particular ministry. It is not one that most of us should covet, though many others will be required to consider that challenge. Where we meet those trying to exercise this ministry, we will need to be both sensitive and patient, fully aware of the tensions that they have to confront.

CHAPTER 10

SEXUAL RELATIONSHIPS, MONEY AND JUDGMENT: HOW DO THEY LOOK TO A LAWYER?

I want to offer three examples of how those of us whose lives are much spent immersed in secular culture may read Scripture with slightly different spectacles to the professional theologian. Inevitably these come from a personal perspective, and I am not saying that even every Christian lawyer would see things this way; indeed, I am sure that they would not. Yet it is just the sort of thing that can only be authentically illustrated from a personal perspective. I am not seeking to persuade any reader to my way of thinking but only making the point that we will all bring to the Scriptures experience accumulated in secular culture, and that may affect our understanding and application of what we read. I would very much want to encourage everyone to think through how this might apply to them whatever their role in whatever culture they are engaged outside the institutional church.

[A] SEXUAL RELATIONSHIPS

I have already acknowledged that my present understanding of sexual relations in Scripture is that God has given sexual intercourse to be expressed between a man and a woman united in the bond of lifelong marriage to the exclusion of all others and for nothing other than that. Whilst my thinking must start from here, it does not dictate or render inevitable all my conclusions.

Sexual relations are only one aspect of loving human relationships. There are very many such relationships, both within family and friendship, which have no sexual element at all. For me, one of the best analyses of this is to be found in C.S. Lewis's book "The Four Loves" — the distinction between affection, sexual attraction, friendship and selfless love ("agape") is very persuasive. Our culture, however, finds it difficult to accept that a close personal relationship between two people not related by blood would not have a sexual element. Moreover, the Scriptural prohibitions on relationships outside marriage are very much focused on the sexual elements: affection, friendship and agape are warmly commended. The contentious aspect of this debate, therefore, focuses on two matters: first, the definition of marriage; and secondly, the place, if any, of sexual intercourse outside that relationship. That seems to be what is in issue.

My acknowledgement inevitably puts me very much on one side of the argument over marriage and sexual relationships that presently so dominates the Christian church — or at least the public perception of it. Yet I have at the same time administered with — as I believe it — integrity a secular system of family law in which that is very much a minority view and in which all are entitled to be treated equally irrespective of sexual orientation. I believe that no one reading a secular judgment of mine would be able to discern my personal views on this subject. That is not because I have compartmentalized my faith or that I am a hypocrite. It is because I believe in and think that we should respect personal choice and personal accountability. Nevertheless, there is then an apparent tension between what I believe and what I do. How, if at all, can that be reconciled? Or if, as may well be the case, it cannot be reconciled, how can that tension be held and managed with integrity?

A good starting point is Jesus' most extended piece of teaching on marriage set out in Matthew.[80] Whilst he recognizes that the Old Testament permits divorce, his teaching is, in reality, uncompromising. It is worth noting his disciples' immediate reaction (v10): "If such is the case of a man with his wife, it is better not to marry." They recognised that this standard is, in practice, almost unattainable. That they may be right about that can be seen by further reflection on the Sermon on the Mount. If we think honestly about Jesus' teaching on adultery,[81] that the one who lusts after another has already committed adultery in the heart, which presumably applies to women as it does to men, there will be few who emerge spotless. Nor should this surprise us when we read Jesus' summary at the end of that chapter: "Be perfect, therefore, as your heavenly Father is perfect."[82] In short, we will all have failed, including those who have only had sexual relations with one partner of the opposite sex within lifelong marriage. We may pass the outward test but, as God reminded Samuel as he sought to discern whom to anoint as king, "The Lord looks on the heart."[83]

All this suggests to me that we should not dilute standards simply because none of us has (or probably could have) attained to them. Secular law must, of course, act differently because, as Jesus recognised in his comment on the Mosaic law, even that must provide a system with which people can reasonably be expected to comply and which therefore must acknowledge the realities of the culture in which it is established. We may have to

---

[80] Matthew 19 v 1–9.
[81] Matthew 5 v 27.
[82] V 48.
[83] I Samuel 16 v 7.

make a distinction between the aspirational — God's standard of perfection — and the practicable — that which can be legally enforced. What Jesus' teaching should do, however, is dramatically affect the tone of the debate.

There is a strong tendency in this area of debate for each of us to divide the world into those who have got it right and those who have not, where we find ourselves necessarily on the side of those who have got it right. However much we may know what is right, we have, in fact, all got it wrong in our lives to some extent. This is not a debate where Christians can stand on one side of the divide shouting at those on the other. Rather it is one where we should huddle together as forgiven sinners under the shadow of the Cross. That does not resolve the debate about the standards required by God or of each other, nor does it resolve the issue of defining marriage, but it does significantly affect the tone in which it is to be conducted. It may also affect the standards that we actually impose on one another as a condition of membership or, more controversially, leadership within the Christian community. It may also have the effect of our considering sexual relations and sexuality in the round rather than isolating for discussion certain individual expressions of it.

We also need to be aware that the forms of single-sex relationships contemplated in the Bible would still stand condemned today because they carried connotations of adultery (as conventionally most adults were married) and, in the Greek world of the New Testament, connotations also of paedophilia. That is because the habit was often to play away from home with young men. The kind of permanent and exclusive relationships contended for today just were not under the specific consideration of the biblical writers. Accordingly, this is not an argument capable of simply being resolved beyond dispute by proof text citation but requires an attempt to understand and apply the principles of biblical teaching. It is at this point that many Christians differ and where we need prayerfully to try to understand the way ahead. I think it is a seriously difficult question. That is why a focus on Jesus' teaching about marriage (and the aspiration to perfection) may be a helpful way in.

Although I must find myself very much on one side of the debate about the definition of marriage, I am not offering a specific answer to what is to be required of church members or church leaders. That has to be worked out, however painfully, by the church as a body. Rather I am making a plea that this fraught debate be conducted in a tone and manner that suggests that in the end we are all on the same side: forgiven sinners trying to live as servants and ambassadors in the places where God has put us. Furthermore, this debate should not be conducted from heavily defended trenches but should be pursued as a journey in which none of us is quite sure where it will end. T.S. Eliot caught the mood —

We shall not cease from exploration

And the end of all our exploring

Will be to arrive where we started

And know the place for the first time.[84]

The practice of family law impresses on anyone involved in it the fallibility of humanity and the pain implicit in divided relationships. It compels us to recognise that people will make decisions with which we may not agree, but those decisions may have to be balanced against the needs of children, extended family and community. If Jesus' teaching be taken literally (as I have concluded that it should), that has as much to say about second marriages (whilst the former partner is still alive) as it

---

[84] Little Gidding: Part V (from the Four Quartets).

does about any other form of sexual relationship. We appear long since to have accepted that second marriages do not disqualify anyone from membership, or even leadership, in the church. The question is whether the logic that led to that requires also to be applied to other forms of relationship. We no longer require of each other the living out of the ideal (from which we all fall short, as I have suggested); the question is where the line is now drawn in terms of membership and leadership of the People of God. How do we handle the tension between the aspirational and our practical fallibility?

It is not my purpose to provide answers. Each must be convinced in their own mind, and the church must find a way ahead. My purposes are a little different. First, it is to say that the aspirational is not to be rejected simply because we cannot attain to it. Neither, of course, may we seek to assert that our lives comply with the aspirational simply because others do not see our fallibilities: that is dangerously near hypocrisy. My second purpose is to contend for a much humbler attitude in this debate. We are, in truth, all sinners and therefore all on the wrong side of perfection. We are fellow seekers after truth. It follows that we must be able to disagree and, if necessary, disagree profoundly, without forfeiting fellowship. Disagreement and conflict may be healthy routes to discerning the truth. Breaking fellowship usually amounts to advancing the purposes of Satan.

[B] MONEY

As Samuel Butler observed, the love of money may be the root of all evil, but the want of money is so quite as truly. Money itself may be morally neutral; it is in its acquisition and use, that moral choices are called into play, and it is those choices in which the

Christian is inescapably involved.

Historically, coinage was worth its face value and was created out of gold, silver, copper and so on. My eighteenth-century purse would have contained metal whose actual value equated to its face value. In modern times we have, in reality, abandoned that kind of money. Now we effectively trade on promissory notes and credit. If you look at the face of a £20 note, you will see the words — "I promise to pay the bearer on demand the sum of twenty pounds." We implicitly trust that promise and so trade with that note as though it were worth its weight in gold. Our whole financial system has trust and reliability as its basis. Thus, whilst money itself may indeed be morally neutral, our use of it necessarily has moral implications and a moral foundation.

I am not here concerned to debate either economic or political theory as a very broad spectrum of both is not inconsistent with Christian faith whilst, in practice, none is fully consistent with it. Economic and political theory is very much concerned with how some goal is achieved; our concerns are much more about concentrating on what those goals are, and achieving that has never been easy.

In the Old Testament law, it is said — "There will, however, be no one in need among you..."[85] That is because if everyone used their wealth rightly, there would be enough for everyone. Yet in the very same chapter, we read — "Since there will never cease to be some in need on the earth..."[86] Or, as Jesus famously acknowledged — "for you always have the poor with you..."[87] That is because humanity has never been able to use wealth rightly. Wrong choices are repeatedly made.

---

[85] Deuteronomy 15 v 4.
[86] v 11.
[87] Matthew 26 v 11.

In trying to look at these choices, I want to concentrate on those that Christians as individuals have to make. How does my use of money fit in with being salt and light, with ambassador, steward or tenant? It is sometimes hard enough to find the right questions to ask, let alone find the right answer to those questions. This is another area of life where a high degree of responsibility is entrusted to the individual Christian by God.

That said, the Bible has a great deal to say about wealth and money over and beyond the fact that the love of money is the root of all kinds of evil.[88] That is as true of the Gospels as anywhere else. Certainly, you will find much more there about money than about sex. That, at the very least, must mean that how we acquire and use wealth and money is a critical aspect of our life and witness as a Christian.

Moreover, both questions matter. Christians have always thought about the use of money, but its acquisition equally raises ethical questions, and I believe that we will have to account for our answers. I am conscious of how much has been written and said about Christians and money; the purpose of this section is no more than to consider how it impacts on individuals in the context of the issues raised in this book.

A Christian may or may not have a substantial influence over their income. Those who inherit money may confront choices over its use, but its acquisition was outside their control. Likewise, when I became a judge, I was paid a salary that was decided by Parliament and publicly advertised. There was a convention that judges did not augment their salary with other earnings except for writing or editing legal books. Some can bargain for salaries (particularly in the private sector), whereas others cannot. When I was a barrister, and thus self-employed, I

---

[88] I Timothy 6 v 10.

had some real influence over my earnings, so my decision to concentrate on the work that I did, necessarily had financial implications. Those with money to invest likewise confront choice when acquiring income and wealth. This is not the place for a detailed discussion of ethical investment; my point is that we will be as accountable for where we invest just as we will be for the use of the fruits of that investment.

There are, however, two more general points that we should note. First, it is essential that money and wealth are honestly acquired. This is an issue as old as money itself. The Old Testament law was clear—

"You shall not cheat in measuring length, weight or quantity. You shall have honest balances, honest weights, an honest ephah and an honest hin...."[89]

When that was disregarded, the prophets were quick to speak, as for example in Micah —

"Can I forget the treasures of wickedness in the house of the wicked, and the scant measure that is accursed? Can I tolerate wicked scales and a bag of dishonest weights?"[90]

Trust and honesty lie not only at the heart of our modern economic system; they are obligations that weigh heavily on every individual Christian choice in the acquisition of income and wealth. Philanthropic use can never justify dishonest acquisition.

The second point is that at the heart of choices to be made is the answer to this question: what has God called me to do? That is the key starting point. If the call is to unpaid work, other questions will arise about self and family support. If it is to paid work in the public sector, the income may be a given but, if in the

---

[89] Leviticus 19 v 35–36.
[90] Micah 6 v 10–11.

private sector, it may be negotiable. Part and parcel of this is the decision whether to work full or part-time in the context of other commitments. However the issues are framed, the central question is the same: to what is it that God has called me? It is important at this point to acknowledge the need to respect individual answers given to that very individual question. Only the one who decides will be accountable, and God may have surprising (to us) reasons for the call. My concern is to see that the question is asked; no more than that.

In one of his Essays, Sir Francis Bacon wrote — "money is like muck, not good except it be spread." I remember whilst at school an elderly clergyman in a sermon saying, "… is like muck; spread over the land they do a power of good but in a heap — oh dear!" He was actually talking about clergy, but it would do for wealth or money, and no doubt Bacon would have approved. What does it mean to spread money around? This question is intended to be personal, not political.

Let us start with basics. Everyone needs to house, feed and clothe themselves and their family. That is not just a human obligation but a Christian one too, as Paul rather tartly observed to Timothy—

"And whoever does not provide for relatives, and especially for family members, has denied the faith and is worse than an unbeliever."[91]

However, even that is not straightforward. There is the quality of food and clothing to be considered. Then there is the question of housing. Do I live where God wants me to, or do I live where I can afford to live? For many, that may not, in fact, be a real choice. However, I remember the late John Stott once lamenting in a sermon at the amount of Christian money tied up

[91] I Timothy 5 v 8.

in what he clearly thought were unnecessarily large mortgages. Were he alive now, I suspect that he would express himself even more strongly. It is a real challenge; perhaps I do not need to live where I could afford to. Then there are questions about private education and private health insurance. I would not presume to offer answers but merely to urge that, in the sight of God, these questions are asked and answered. Our way of life cannot simply be assumed because it is the way of life assumed in the culture in which we happen to live.

For our family, these questions effectively answered themselves once we had resolved to respond to God's call to live in inner Liverpool. Housing was cheap; we started in a redundant vicarage as the only owner-occupiers in the parish. Because of a compulsory purchase order some twelve years later, we had to swap our redundant vicarage for what had become the offices of a taxi repair business, which is where we lived for the next thirty-five years.[92] I should perhaps acknowledge that this building was originally (and is now) a double fronted, fourteen-room, Georgian terrace house!

To be effective members of the community, we needed to use local schools and health centres. We remembered Abraham and Isaac and God's covenant love to Isaac even as they approached the mountain of proposed sacrifice. The key question, of course, is: where has God called me to live? The answer to that is probably the key to answering many of the questions raised above. How often, though, is that question actually asked?

Once all the basics are dealt with, which include, of course, the cost of working (travel, clothing and so on), then there is the question of what to do with the rest, if indeed there is anything left. I understand that an analysis of the Torah (the Old Testament

---

[92] We have since downsized to another part of Liverpool.

law) shows that a faithful Jew was obliged to give away at least one-third of his income before a free-will offering could even be considered. Much of that would have been for what is now covered by taxation save that the obligation to support the formal Ministry of the Tabernacle or, later, the Temple would have been included. Clearly, Christians have a strong obligation to shoulder their fair share of the cost of their church and fellowship. Many Christians teach tithing; I am not quite persuaded that that is a Christian obligation even as a minimum. My own view is that the use of money is governed by principle rather than arithmetic.

The best and most direct guidance on this comes from Paul and is found in II Corinthians 8 and 9. The basic principle is this:

"Each of you must give as you have made up your mind, not reluctantly or under compulsion, for God loves a cheerful giver."[93]

We are back again to the responsibilities that God entrusts to us, his stewards. We must not only decide on how to use that money but on how much we allot to each matter. Most of us have to balance quality of food and clothes with outings and holidays, the type of car, if any, and what we are willing to give away.

As we seek the balance, Paul has this to say —

"I do not mean that there should be relief for others and pressure on you, but it is a question of a fair balance between your present abundance and their need, so that their abundance may be for your need, in order that there may be a fair balance. As it is written, 'the one who had much did not have too much, and the one who had little did not have too little'."[94]

It was from this passage that the Christian slogan of thirty years ago derived: Enough is enough. Of course, we should have

---

[93] Corinthians 9 v 7.
[94] Corinthians 8 v 13–15.

enough; it is the balance we must decide about. Nevertheless, hidden in that is the difficult question: what is enough? Within my professional group, I would be seen as one who lives modestly and would have been seen as a barrister as a modest earner. In the context of where we live in Liverpool, I am distinctly rich. When I am in Blantyre with our project, the differences are staggering. So what is enough? Once again, it is a decision that is a matter of personal responsibility before God to whom we must answer. What counts is that we ask the question.

In the passage referred to, Paul is keen that we should understand that generosity blesses the one who gives as well as the one who receives; many Christians will bear witness to the truth of that. The essence of giving, therefore, is not arithmetic but love: our grateful response to the love of God for us and our loving response to those in need, as the love of God overflows in our hearts. Of course, arithmetic has a place as we work out our decisions, but the motivation for them is love.

I fully recognise that not all will see themselves in all of this. Given where we have lived and the demands made on our time, we have always had enough and usually rather more. Others who follow God's call may find that their financial circumstances are very different. I have found the responsibility of having more than we need onerous and exhilarating: onerous because it is a real pressure trying to do right, exhilarating because it is a real privilege to be able to give.

My impression is that those who seek to live as ambassadors and faithful stewards face two basic challenges over money. The first is direct: what does it mean to have enough? For each person, the answer will be different, but the question must be confronted. The second is less direct but equally important: what has God called me to do — where to work and live? Our answer to that will affect deeply our thinking about our own financial resources. Yet however much these things must be thought through (and it is vital that they are), in the end, this is not a cerebral issue but is a true witness to the love that we have within us.

[C] JUDGMENT

Any judge sitting in the pew in the modern Western church is likely to be surprised at how little is heard from the pulpit about judgment, considering how much both Old and New Testament have to say about it. You simply cannot fairly read the scriptures, and in particular the Gospels, without appreciating that judgment lies near the heart of it. If the Bible from Genesis 12 onwards is the story of God's rescue plan, his salvation, then there must come a time of judgment, a time when everything is set to rights, a time for determining who or what is to be part of the new heaven and the new earth. Now judgment is a matter for the perfect justice of God tempered by his love of mercy, and we would be wise not to be drawn too easily into second-guessing his purposes by substituting our own fallible judgments.

However, we can perhaps be clear about two matters. His promise is that through the death and resurrection of Jesus, all who believe in him will indeed belong to God forever. This is not because we deserve it, for then, as a late and lamented friend used to remark, heaven would be a veritable "prigsty", but because God has chosen to love us and adopt us as his children. Secondly, we can perhaps be sure that God will not impose his love unasked or unwanted on any human: that is the consequence of the terrifying privilege of human freedom. Beyond that, I would want to be very cautious.

That said, I have always found instinctively compelling the idea that the final judgment will, in effect, be self-selecting. It is most beautifully caught in one of the final scenes in CS Lewis's "The Last Battle". As the created order rushes towards the Great Lion, he writes—

"And all of these ran up to the door where Aslan stood... The creatures came rushing in... but as they came right up to Aslan, one or other of two things happened to each of them. They all looked straight in his face, I don't think they had any choice about that. And when some looked, the expression on their faces changed terribly — it was fear and hatred... and all the creatures that looked at Aslan that way swerved to their right and disappeared into his huge... Shadow... But the others looked in the face of Aslan and loved him, though some of them were very frightened at the same time."

The echo of Jesus' parable of the sheep and goats[95] is there of course, but there is a slightly different emphasis. Our choices in life have conditioned our ultimate response to Jesus, and in that we shall be our own judges.

It is for me inconceivable that history can have any conclusion that does not involve judgment. It is judgment that validates what is right and good. That judgment is about the setting of all things to right and is an indispensable element not only of the love of God (as well as his Holiness) but also of the perfection of the new creation.

As I say, an air of humility and caution is welcome where we engage in what is ultimately a matter for God. Of course, our ultimate destiny is a matter of supreme importance on which (unlike perhaps in the modern Western church) preachers, theologians and teachers have had much to say. I do not think that

---

[95] Matthew 25 v 31–48.

I can usefully add further to that — save perhaps in one matter.

You cannot read the New Testament, and the teachings of Jesus in particular, without concluding that each of us will have to give an account of our lives. Although many Christians find it uncomfortable, especially those of us raised in a Protestant culture, Jesus talks as freely of rewards as of punishment. This is at its clearest in the Parable of the Talents, though, for me, his oddest comment is what he says in an earlier passage:

"And whoever gives even a cup of cold water to one of these little ones in the name of a disciple — truly, I tell you, none of these will lose their reward."[96]

There seems to me here to be something at work that is distinct from the awesome drama of final judgment. However much a believer may be secure in the love of God in that event, there is still an account to be given, for joy or sorrow (perhaps inevitably both), for the life we have actually lived. And would we really want it otherwise, for it is this giving of an account that establishes meaning to our lives and its significance in the eyes of God?

The nearest that I have got to understanding this is through some words of Paul where he writes:

"Now if anyone builds on this foundation with gold, silver, precious stones, wood, hay, straw — the work of each builder will become visible, for the day will disclose it, because it will be revealed with fire and the fire will test what sort of work each has done. If what is being built on the foundation survives, the builder will receive a reward. If the work is burned, the builder will suffer loss; the builder will be saved but only as through fire."[97]

---

[96] Matthew 10 v 42.
[97] I Corinthians 3 v 13–15.

I do not think it helpful (nor indeed am I remotely competent) to speculate on how or when this might happen. It simply seems to me both that justice demands that we should give an account of the stewardship of our lives and also that through the love of God, expressed through our adoption, we should be his forever. The two are complementary, not contradictory. How exactly they are worked out and how they interact may make for fascinating speculation, but the wise Christian is probably content to leave those matters alone.

One of the difficulties that many Western Christians have in thinking about judgment is that we are hooked on the picture of the criminal court. In that court, punishment may be found but rarely reward. Judgment is to be feared, whereas in the eyes of the New Testament, this judgment of believers may be as much about joy as sorrow, although for most of us it will probably involve both. We will see beautiful consequences of our life of which we had not an inkling; an act of love or generosity, long forgotten by us, is revealed with all its effects.

I have in this respect found very helpful CS Lewis's "Reflection on the Psalms" (Chapter 2). It is surprising to discover the Psalmist imploring God's judgment on himself — for his vindication; we find similar demands in the book of Job. That is because the Psalmist is using the picture of the civil court in which one seeks to have a wrong put right — as in Jesus' story of the importunate widow and the unjust judge.[98] The biblical writers could envisage judgment to joy as much as judgment to sorrow. The picture of the criminal cringing in the dock may have its place, but the biblical picture of judgment is much wider than that. Our lives really can rejoice the heart of God and we shall discover that that is so.

---

[98] Luke 18 v 1–8.

What does seem crucial to me, as a Christian judge reflecting on these matters, is that as Christians, we need to be willing to confront the reality of judgment as an experience through which all must pass and then to embrace these two complementary strands of God's justice. The first strand is that I will be required to account for the stewardship of my life. The second is that, whatever may befall, I will belong to God forever. In this way, we may banish both complacency and terror: God desires neither for his adoptive family.

EPILOGUE

THE SALT OF THE EARTH?

I have, in effect, bet my whole life on the truth of the Christian story, on Jesus being who he said that he was. This book merely reflects how that has been worked out. The true value of that life will only be evident when finally, I give an account to God for it. That will be equally true of any other Christian who takes up his cross in the same way and journeys through our Western culture. Should this book shed any light on that journey, I will have had my reward.

All that said, it is right to acknowledge that much good may come in such a journey. When I retired in 2013, I took an eight-day retreat at Scargill House. My hope was to gain insight into retired life. God had another agenda, and I never got as far as the future. The time was consumed in reflection on what had gone before, on both the (painfully) slow journey from who I am to the one God wants me to be (still uncompleted) and also on how God's hand had steered my specific vocation whether I was aware of that at the time or not. It also involved reflection on what is potentially a very painful question: had I spent my time usefully in the sight of God and others?

Two things struck me powerfully. The first was a sense of extraordinary privilege and gratitude for all the opportunities that I had had and for all that had been entrusted to me, even where I had to recognise my mixed success in it all. The second was a sense that God was (surprisingly to me) somewhat indifferent to all my failings. It is that that encourages me to commend to fellow Christians a life in which risks may be taken and where the possibility of error, real enough in itself, is simply an aspect of the normal Christian life. Fear of error must never be allowed to paralyze life.

My aspiration is that every Christian called into this sort of service as an ambassador, to serve as salt and light in God's world, will find their own way of being an effective witness to and servant of Jesus Christ. I have sought to share some of the things that have helped me in that life. Nevertheless, I remain only too aware that so much of what I have written smacks of servanthood rather than sonship, and that others may find that difficult.

I find myself again and again hoping to hear those words, "Well done, good and faithful servant." Indeed for me, perhaps the greatest encomium would be the words of the Fat Controller: "Now you are a Really Useful Engine!" I am not going to weary my reader with any analysis of why this might be so, though I have theories enough of my own. However, I would want to assert two matters. The first is that I delight where others have found a better living balance between knowing themselves first as a child of God and then as his servant. The second is that both are inseparable in the normal Christian life: you cannot have one without the other. As ever the Psalmist has it in one in the very short psalm — 131:

"Oh Lord, my heart is not lifted up, my eyes are not raised too high; I do not occupy myself with things too great and too marvellous for me. But I have calmed and quieted myself, like a weaned child with its mother; my soul is within me like a weaned child. O Israel, hope in the Lord from this time on and for evermore."

I hope that I may be allowed to finish with two personal comments as I look back over a life most of which presumably now lies in the past, and as I look forward into a world in which new generations are being and will be called to serve God in the culture of the Western world. These are offered in the hope of encouraging those called also to walk this way.

The first is that I would have missed none of this for anything. Of course, there have been things done or not done and said or not said that I regret. There will also no doubt be errors shown of which I was not aware or even where I was convinced that I was right. How could it be otherwise with any human life? That said, I have felt overwhelmed by the undeserved privilege of opportunity for service coupled with my own experience (often after the event!) of the love of God. Although, of course, the normal Christian life will be different in day-to-day practice for each one, I believe that many serious Christians, who have had a lifetime's exposure to our secular culture, would be able to share that assessment.

We may well not see how our lives have advanced the purposes of God, but we may have come to share Oscar Romero's confidence that we will, in fact, have done so and that we will come to understand how in the future. We may not fully see how our lives have greatly advanced God's *Shalom*, but Jesus' promise remains that he will give us peace though not as the world gives it.[99] It really was all worth it.

My second personal comment is that I am surprisingly optimistic about the future prospects for Christians who find themselves called to this area of service. I have no doubt that Christians will be needed and, for all the reasons I have given in

---

[99] John 14 v 27.

this book, the task will be no easier than it is now, nor our vocation itself any easier to discern. It will, however, remain of the first importance in the evangelization of future generations that Christians are found to serve as salt and light in our Western culture, which shows no sign of becoming any more open to religious faith than it is now.

I am, however, rather less optimistic about the ability of the institutional church to adapt to this challenge. I do very much welcome the recent report from the Archbishops' Council entitled "Setting God's People Free." I hope that this book reflects the spirit of that report. In particular, I welcome their recognition that "What is needed, first and foremost, is not a programme but a change of culture." The report is addressed to the church, whereas this book is addressed to individual laypeople. Given the present demands on the leadership of the church, I am not convinced that they are ready to make this cultural shift. The fact that the report makes points that have often been made over the last century suggests that urgency may not be a feature of that response. I do not believe that as the ambassadors of Christ to this culture, we can simply wait for this to happen; we are called to be his witnesses now.

There will, of course, be opposition and even resentment, and that sadly may not be confined to those who do not share our faith. On the other hand, the sense of balance and ethical priorities that Christians can bring to the conflicts within our culture is likely to prove very valuable and indeed necessary. As ambassadors whose security is firmly established elsewhere, we can commit ourselves to the issues that trouble our culture. We are allowed to take risks, and we may embrace the possibility of error. I shall be surprised if there is not a significant contribution to be made. Just as the presence of ten just people would have saved Sodom and just as the presence of the exiles brought blessing to Babylon, so the presence of Christian salt and light in our culture are the means by which God now blesses the world he created, the world he loves and the world which in due time will be recreated in perfect order. "See," says God. "I am making all things new"[100]. It will indeed be very good, and all those adopted children of God, who sought faithfully to serve, will be part of it.

---

[100] Revelation 21 v 5.

BIBLIOGRAPHY

All quotations from the Bible are taken from the *New Revised Standard Version* (the Canterbury Press)

References to the articles of the ECHR are to those as set out in the Human Rights Act 1998

W. Audrey, *Thomas the Tank Engine et al* (Harper Collins)

Kenneth Bailey, *Jesus through Middle Eastern Eyes* (SPCK), *Paul Through Mediterranean Eyes* (SPCK)

Harry Blamires, *The Christian Mind* (Regent College Vancouver), *The Secularist Heresy* (SPCK)

Jonathan Burnside, *God, Justice & Society* (OUP)

Roger Dowley, *The Lost Bequest* (ECUM)

T.S. Eliot, *Collected Poems* (Faber & Faber)

Robert Harris, *The Cicero Trilogy* (Arrow Books)

Mark Hedley, *The Modern Judge* (LexisNexis)

Bruce Kendrick, *Come Out the Wilderness* (Fontana Books)

C.S. Lewis, *Reflections on the Psalms* (Fount), *The Four Loves* (Fount), *The Last Battle* (Collins)

Ian McEwan, *The Children Act* (Jonathan Cape)

David McIlroy, *A Biblical View of Law & Justice* (Paternoster Press)

John Taylor, *The Go-Between God* (SCM Press)

William Wilberforce, *A Practical View of Christianity* (Republished by Hendrickson's Christian Classics)

Christopher Wright, *Old Testament Ethics* (IVP)

N.T. Wright, *Paul and the Faithfulness of God* (SPCK)